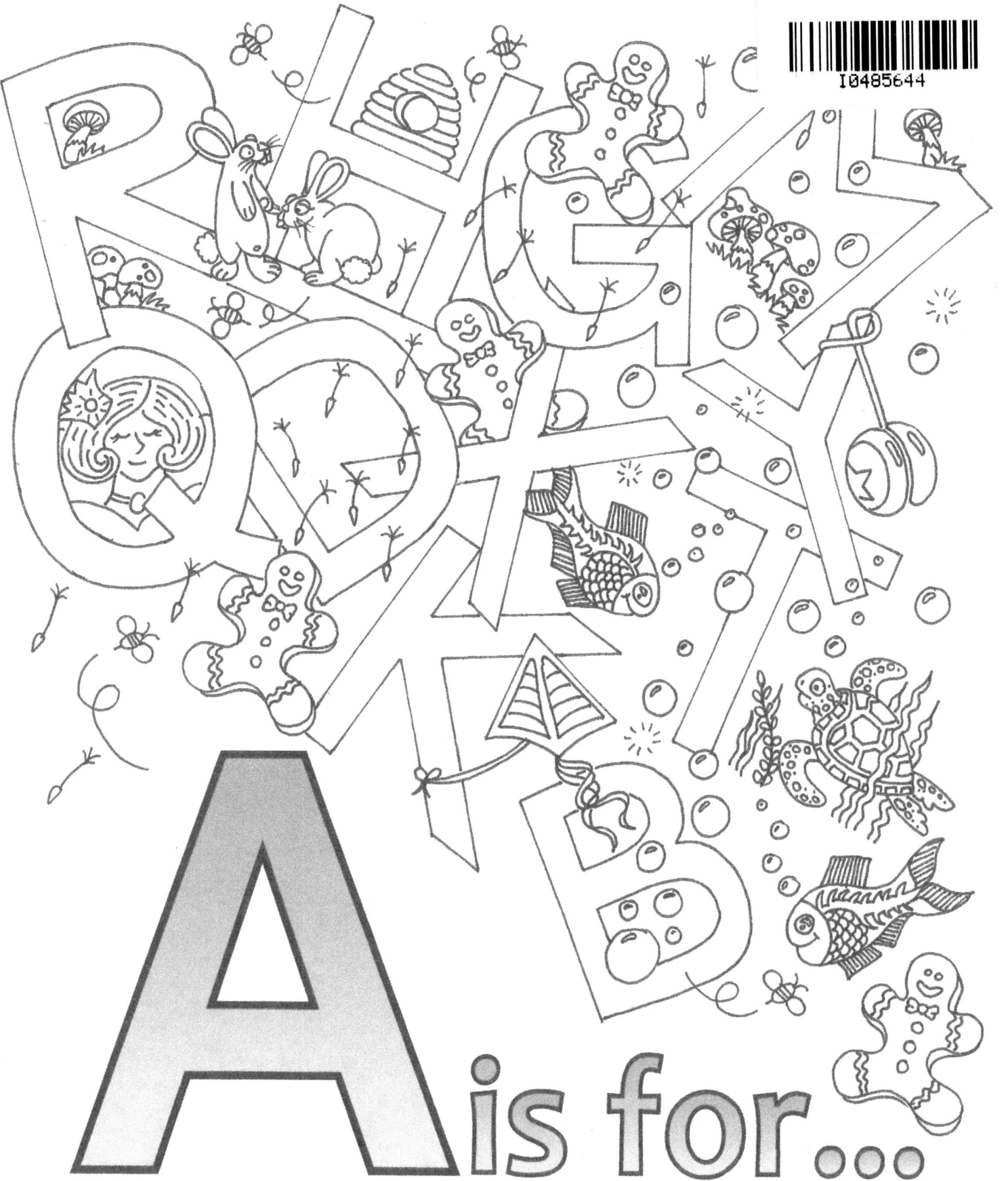

A is for...

An alphabet word search coloring book for all ages!

-TJW Creations

I0485644

About this book....

Hello Colorists!

Here is a little history about the creation of this book.

It was originally created for my 2 young boys, to help with learning the alphabet in a fun way. When I began showing what I was doing to friends and family they suggested I needed to think bigger than just my two boys... It has since morphed into the beautiful book you are holding here today.

It was originally designed to be double sided. I, then came to discover, how much the colorists hated that (especially if you use markers as your primary coloring tool) therefor I have developed some simple pages in between the main coloring pages as a place to write out your "word" finds, or not worry if there is any bleed through from markers or pens, or even color if you so desire! I have also included a color test page but would still suggest using a blotter page between pages if you plan on using markers as your main way to bring life to the "words".

I challenge you to find all the themes I have used though-out! What things can you find that show up throughout the whole book? Can you find all the words I have drawn for each letter? Can you find all the words depicted on the cover ?
~hint A to Z are represented inside the book and no new "words" were used!

I have included a answer sheet at the back, for what I believe are all the words depicted.

I hope you enjoy this book as much as I enjoyed creating it!

Be Happy, Be Calm and Color On!

>   – Tammara Wright
>   TJW Creations

TESTER PAGE...

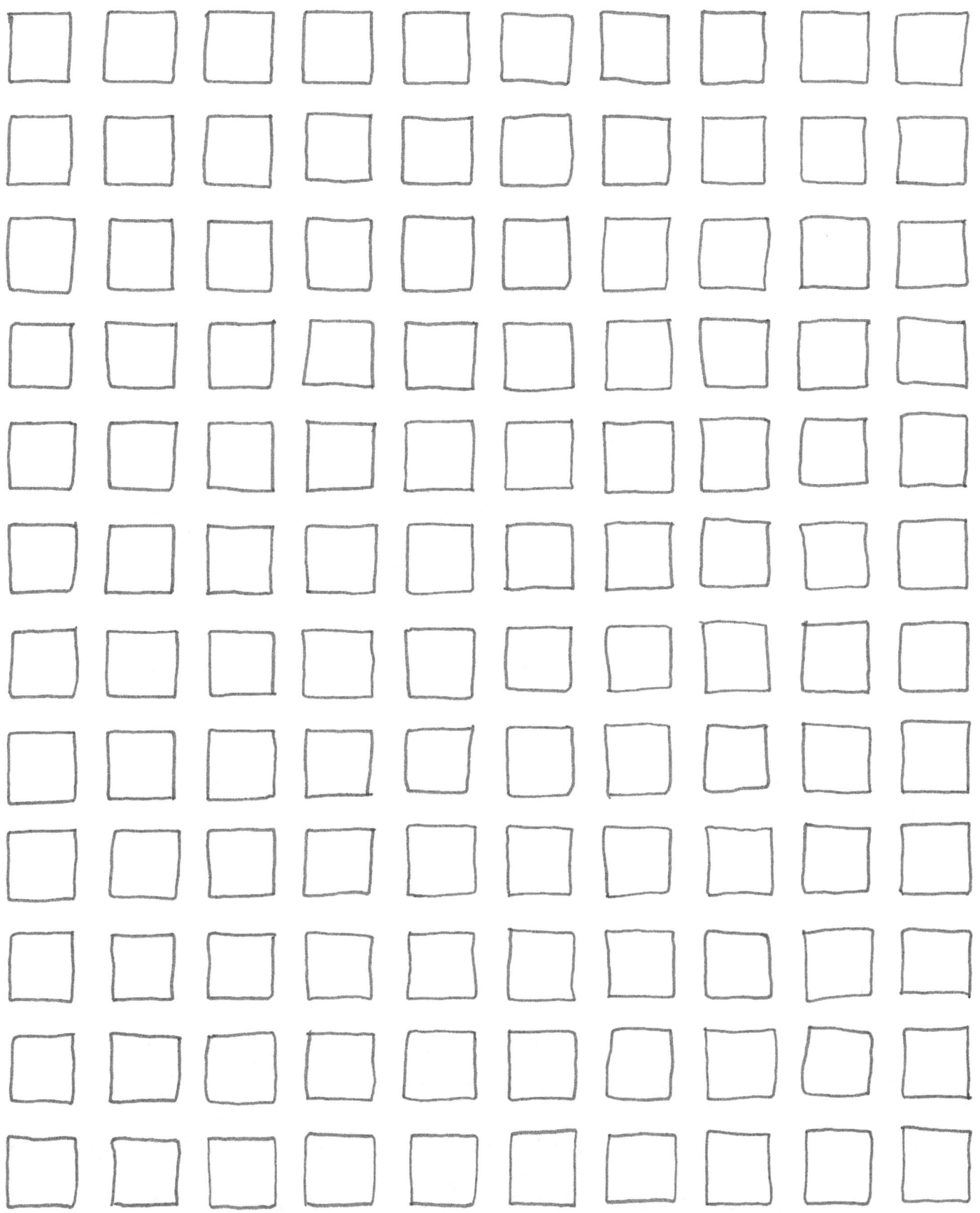

TESTER PAGE...

(You can use this space to test for bleed though, and color swatches)

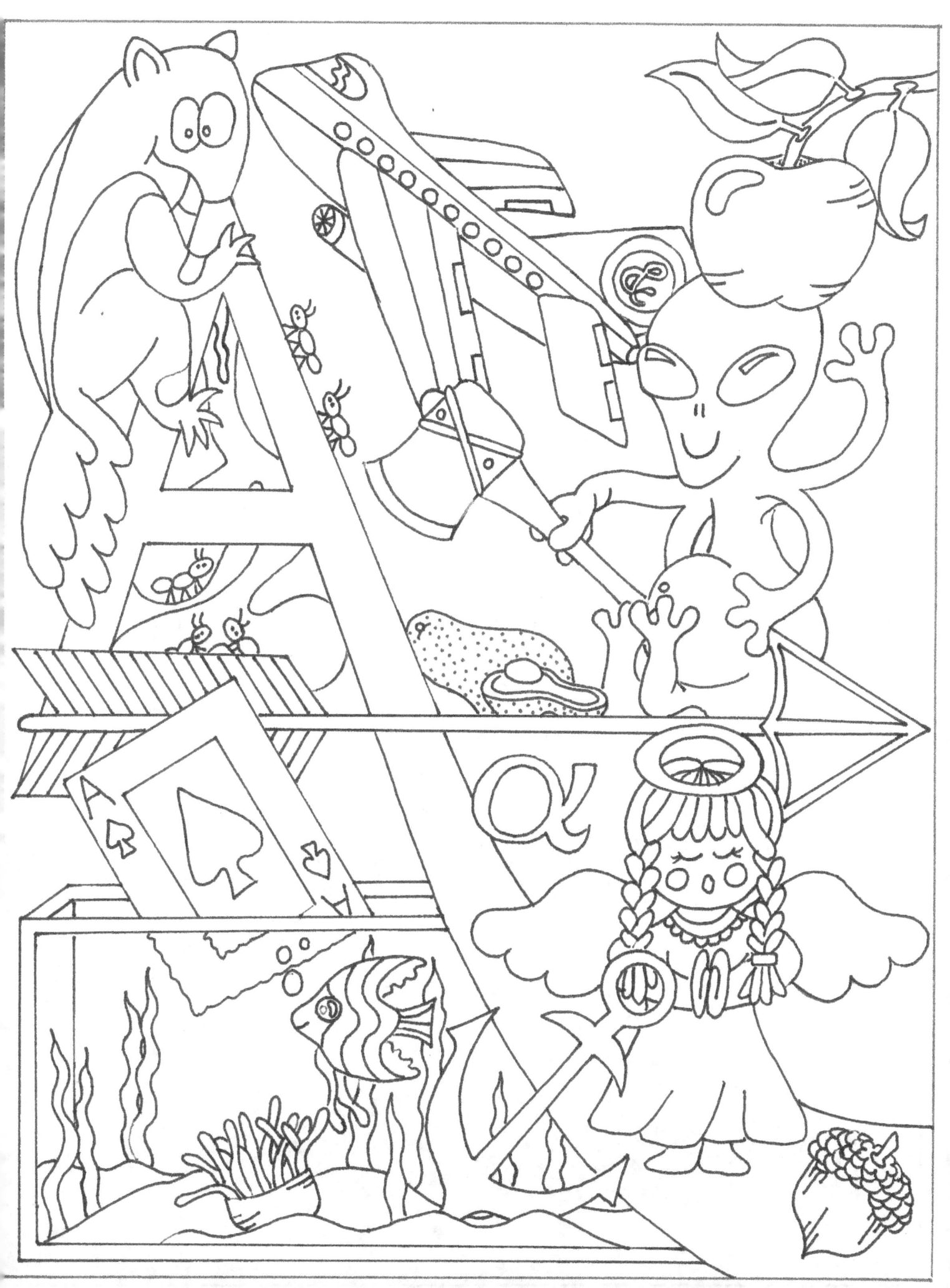

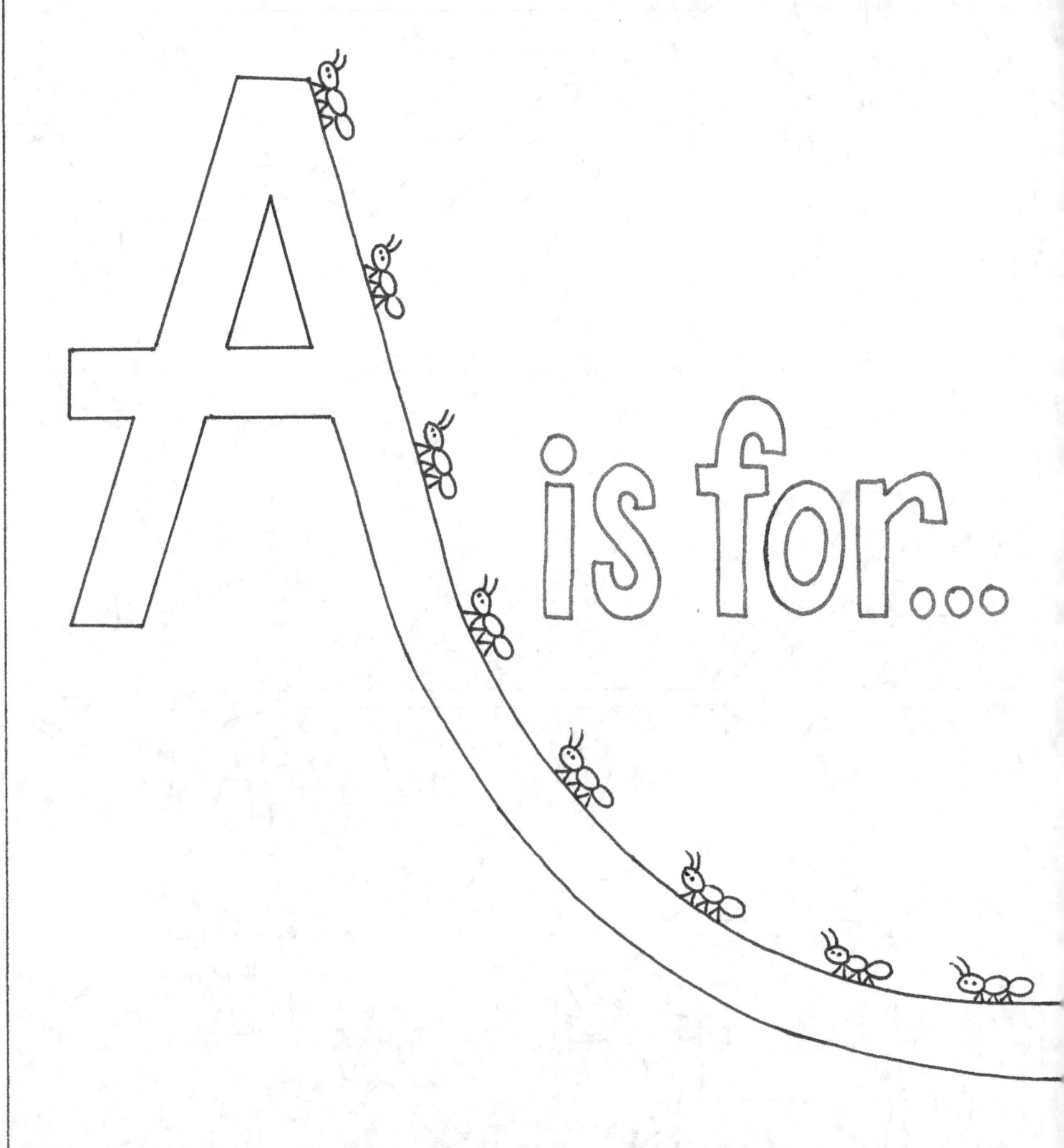

A is for...

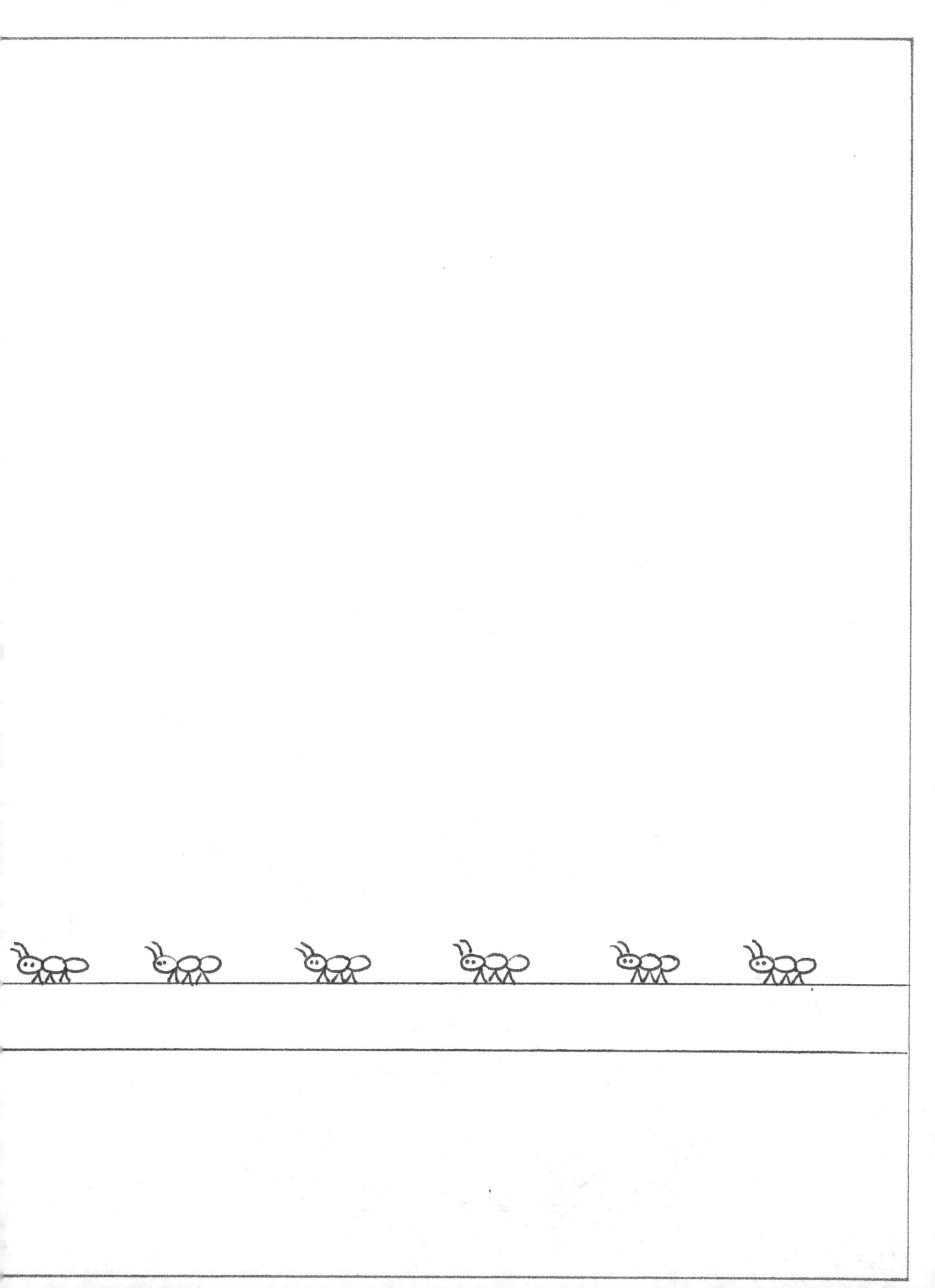

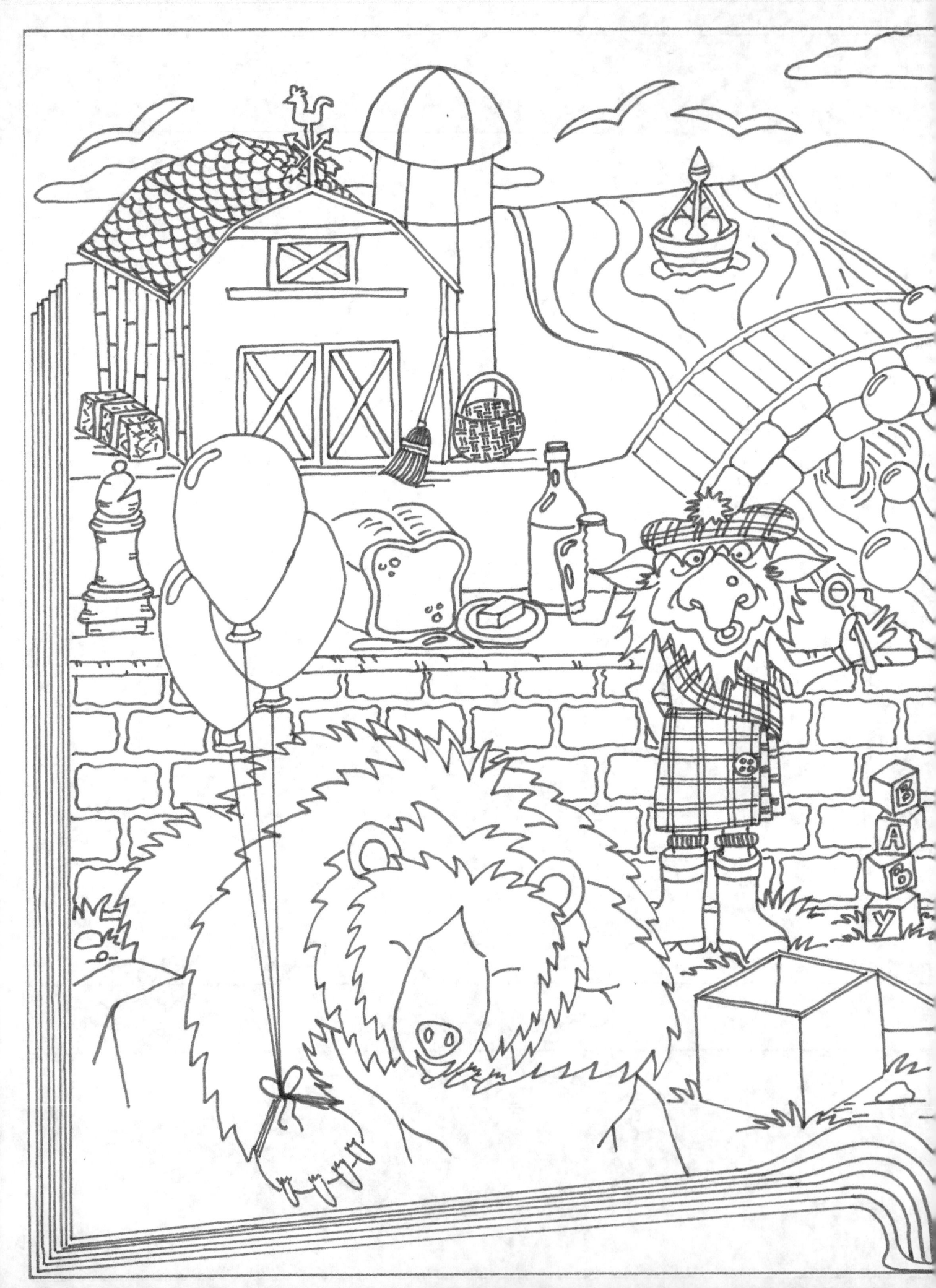

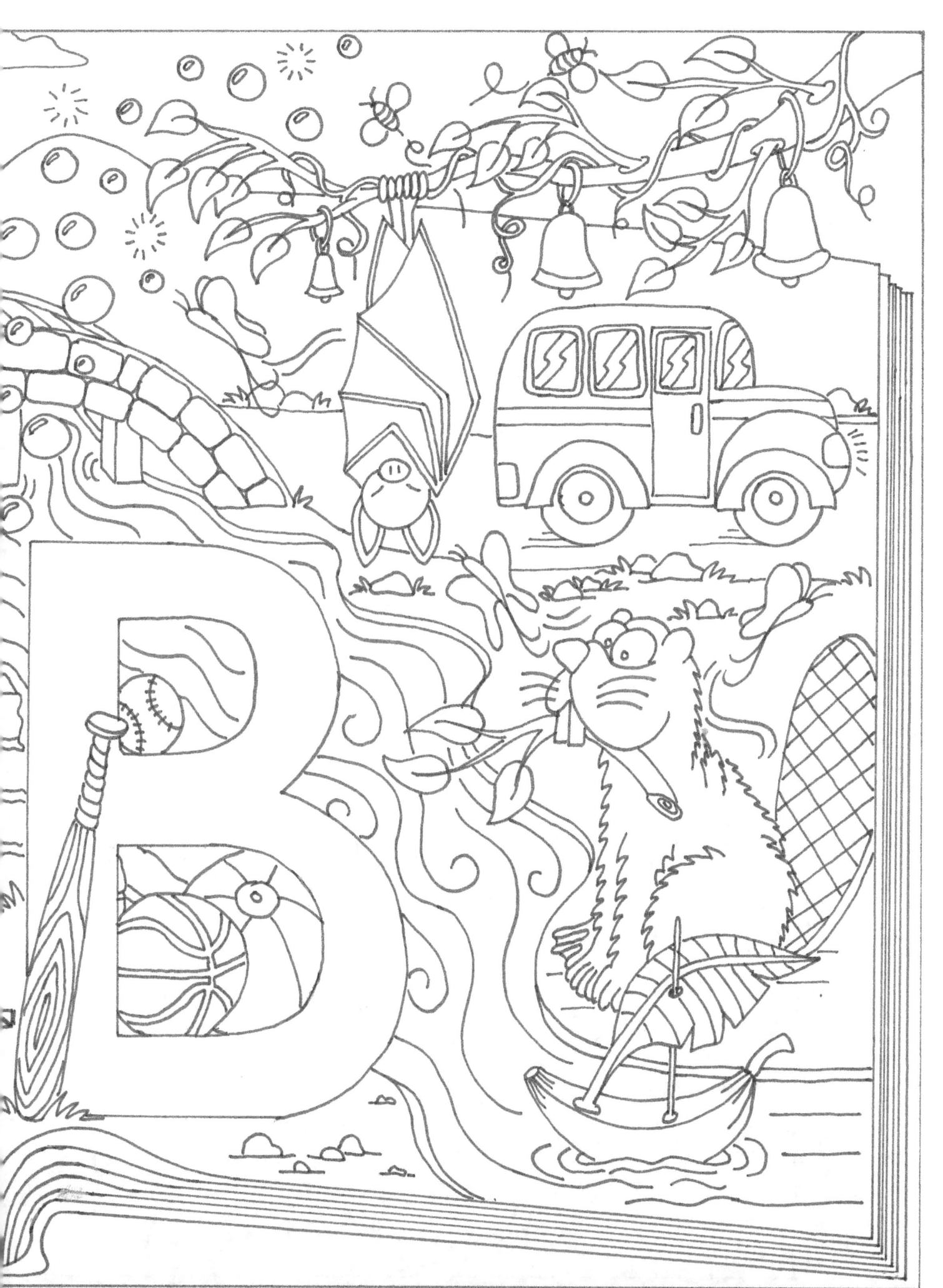

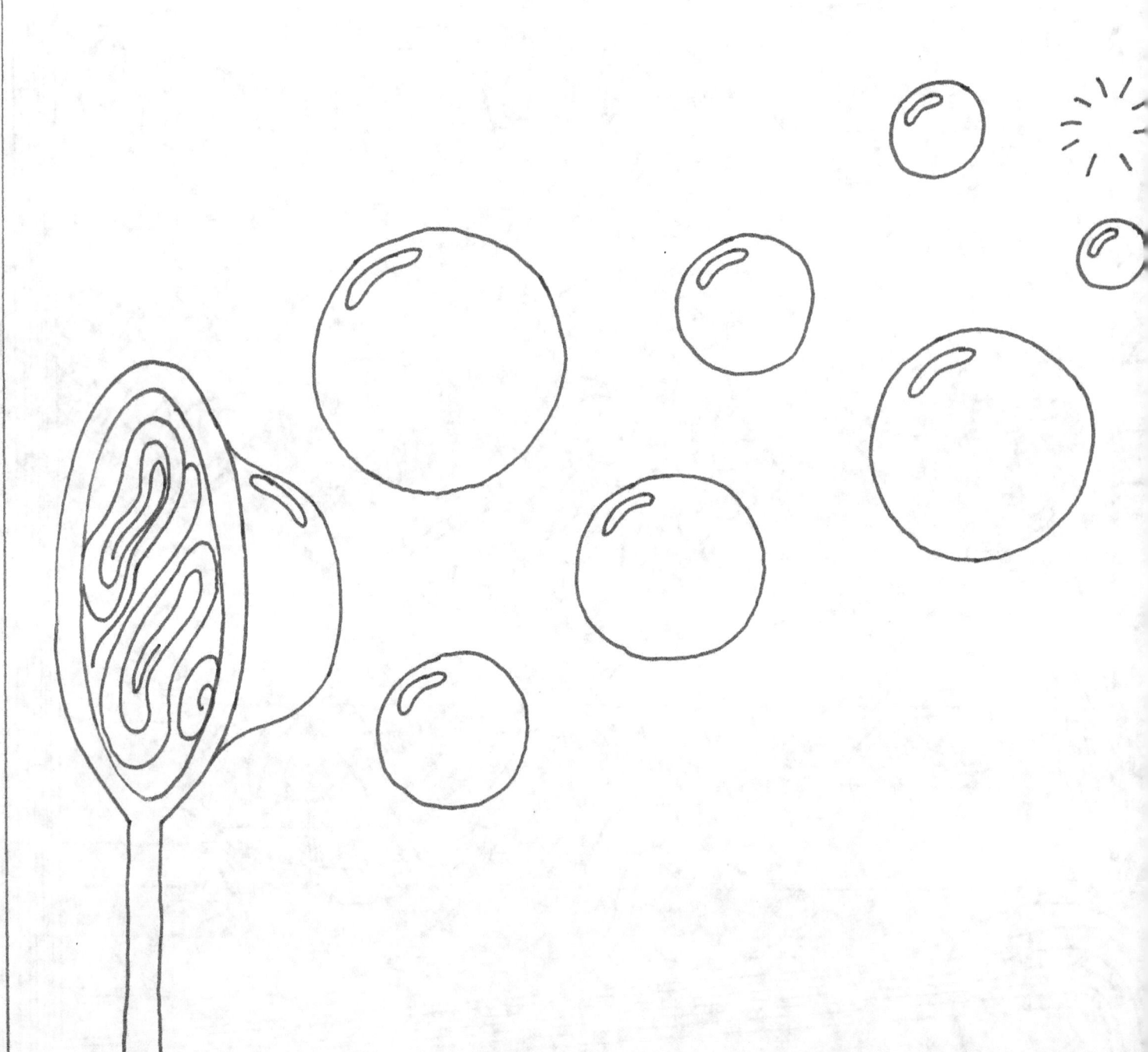

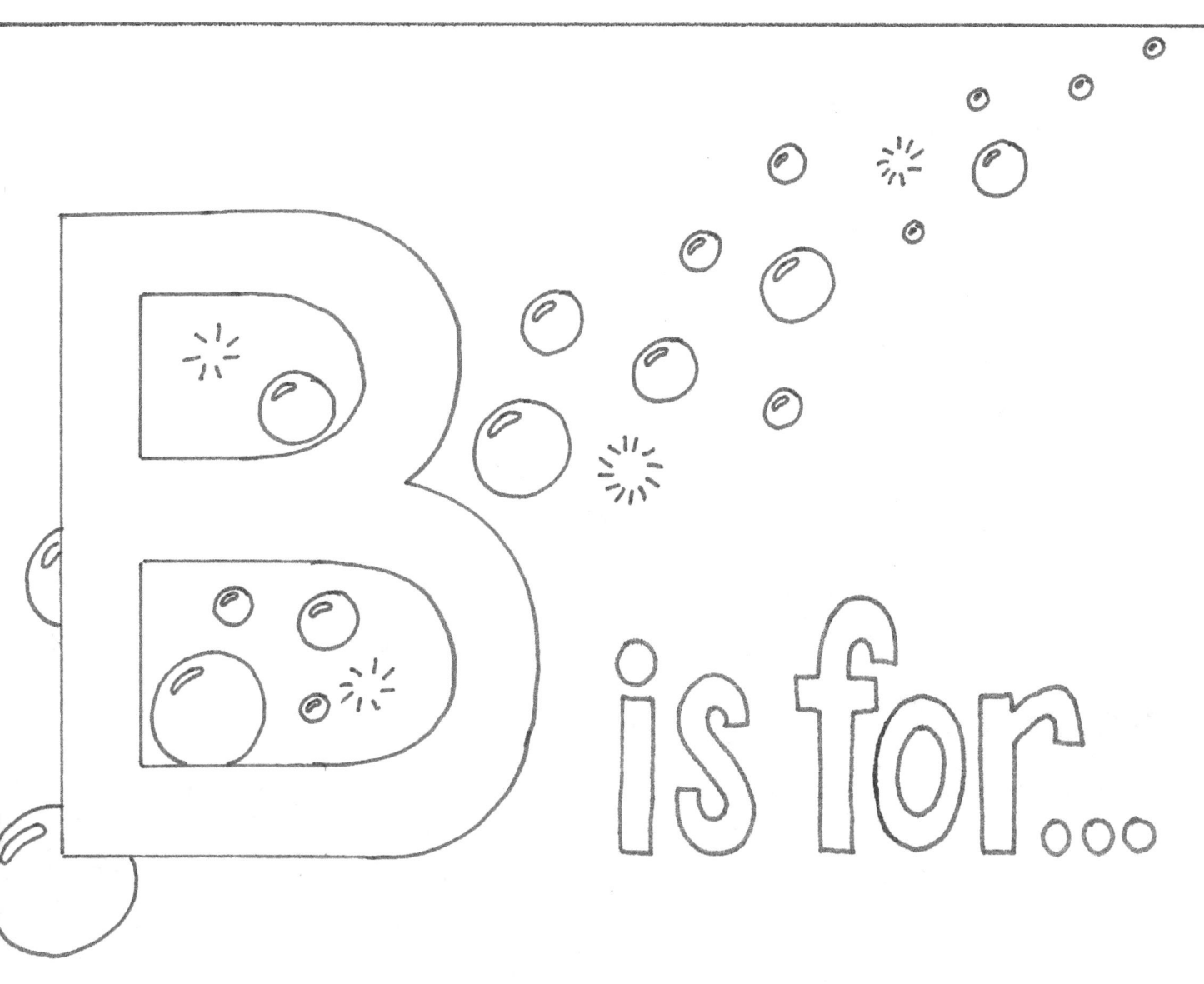

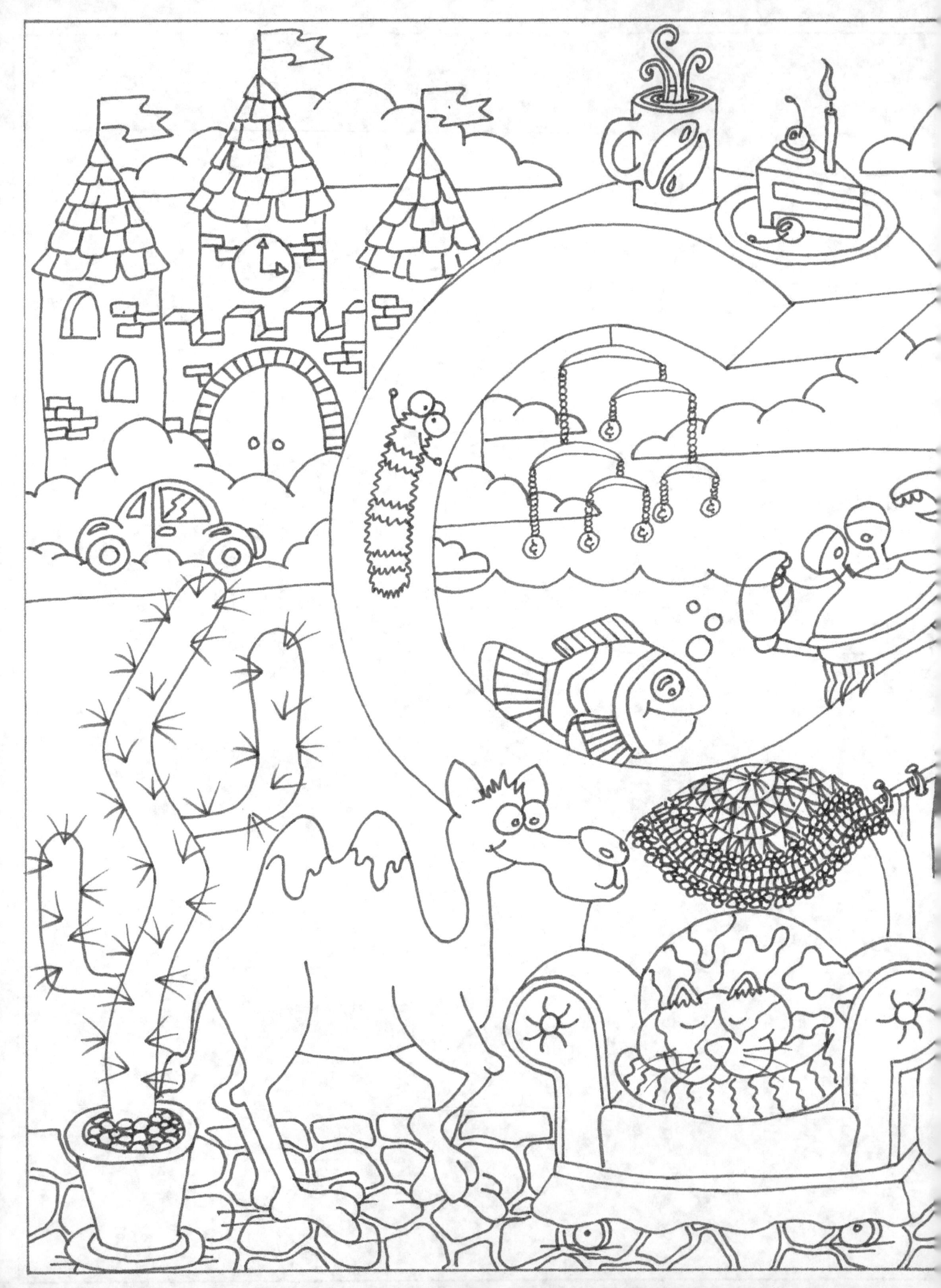

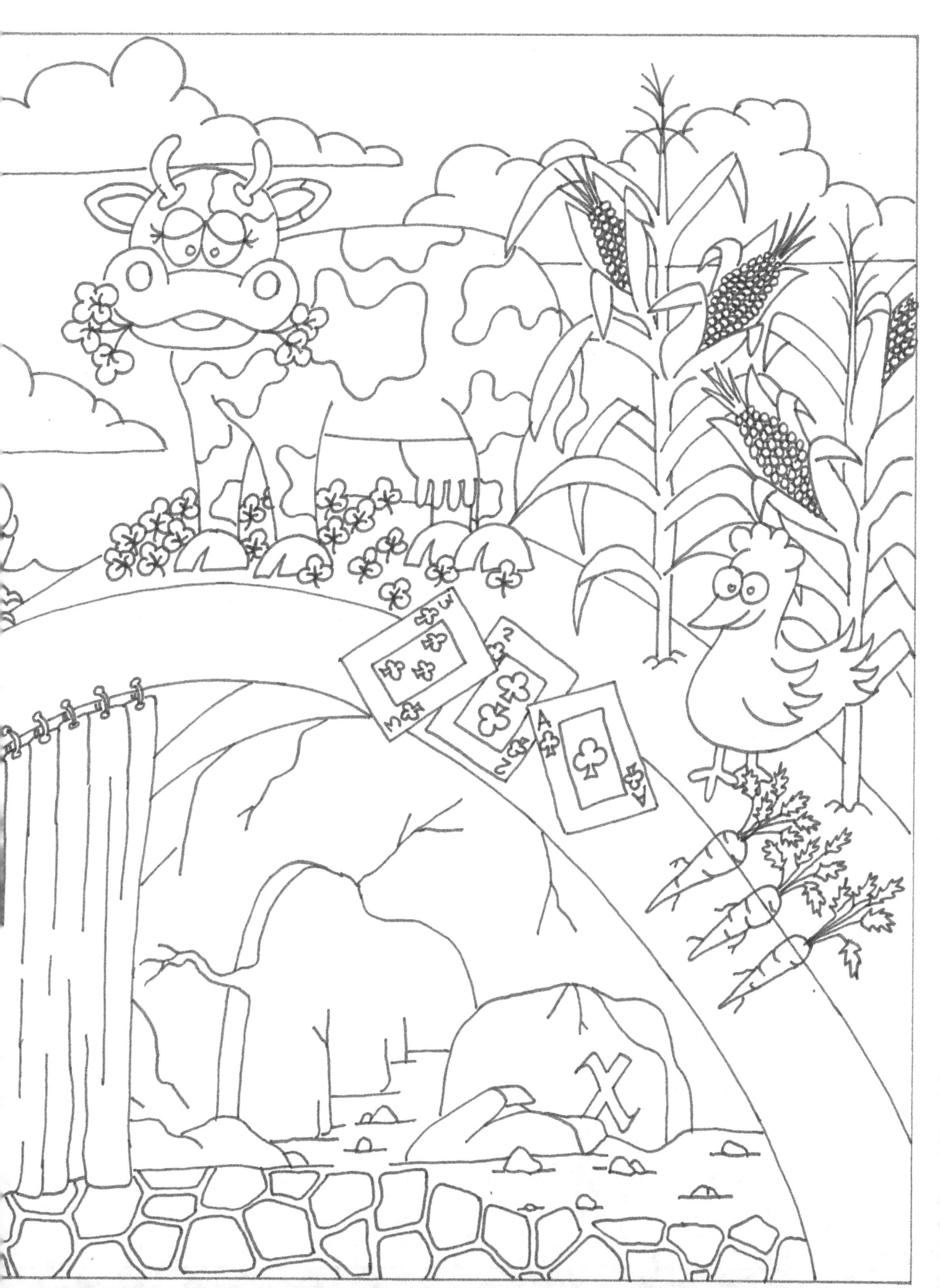

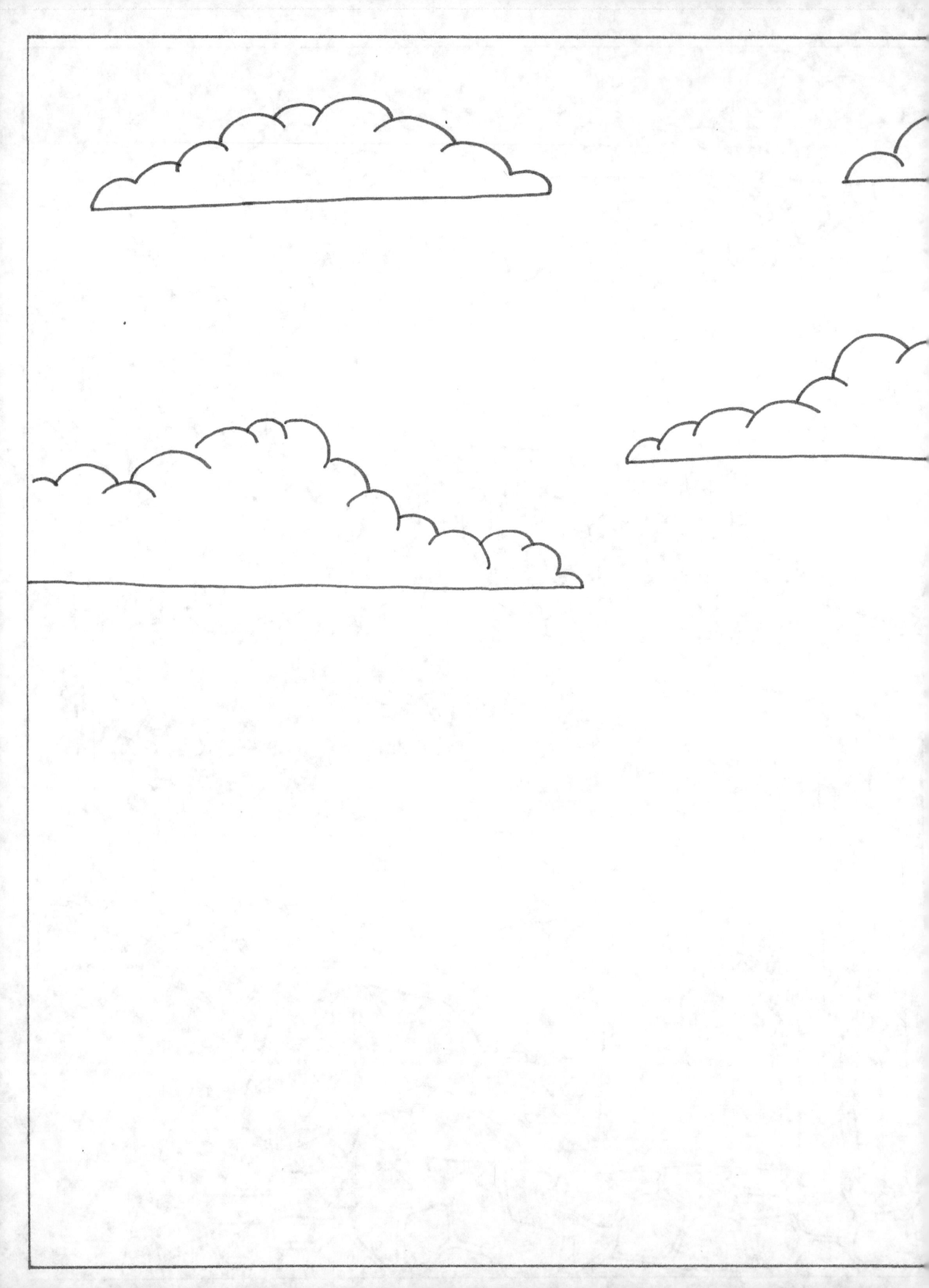

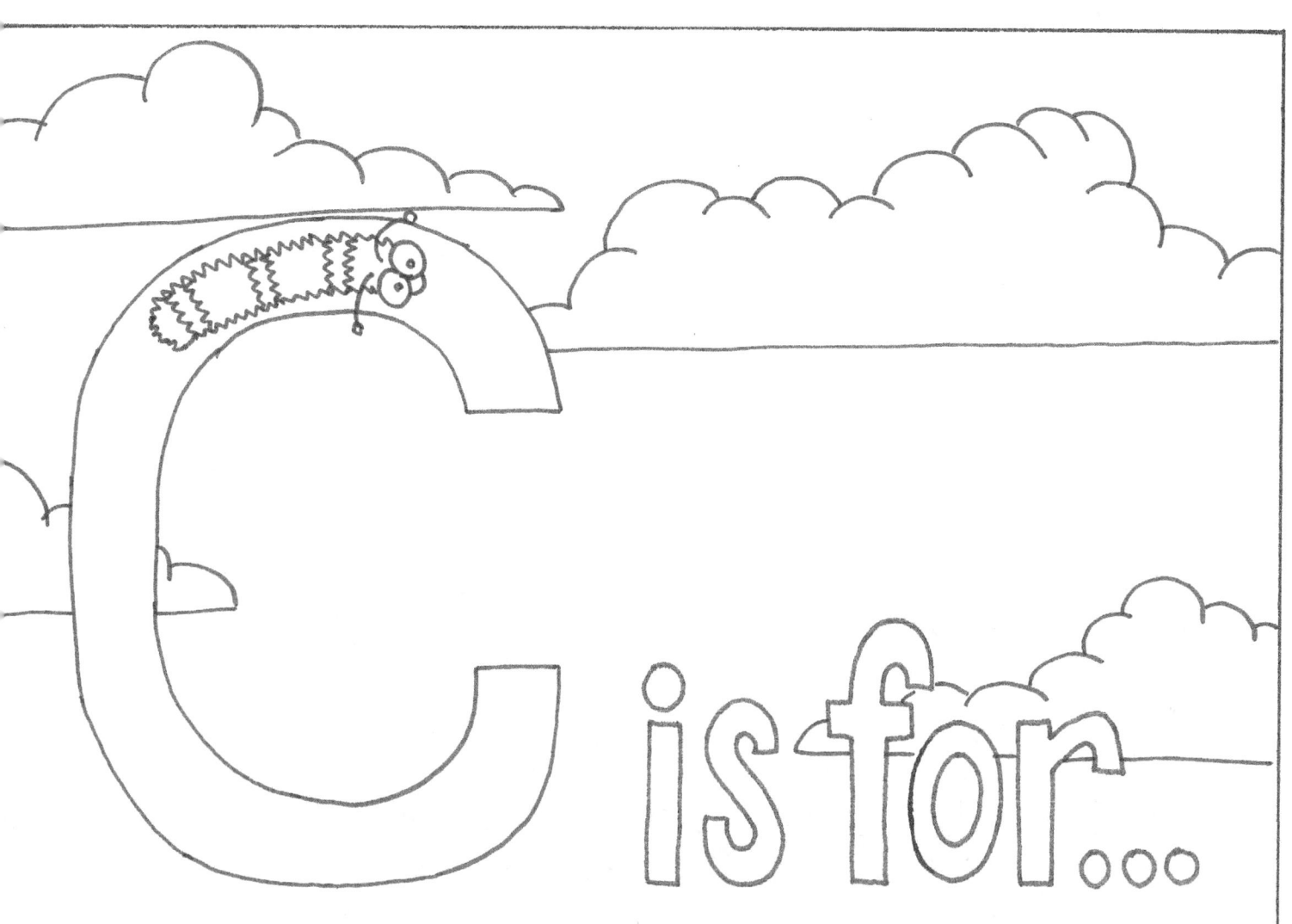

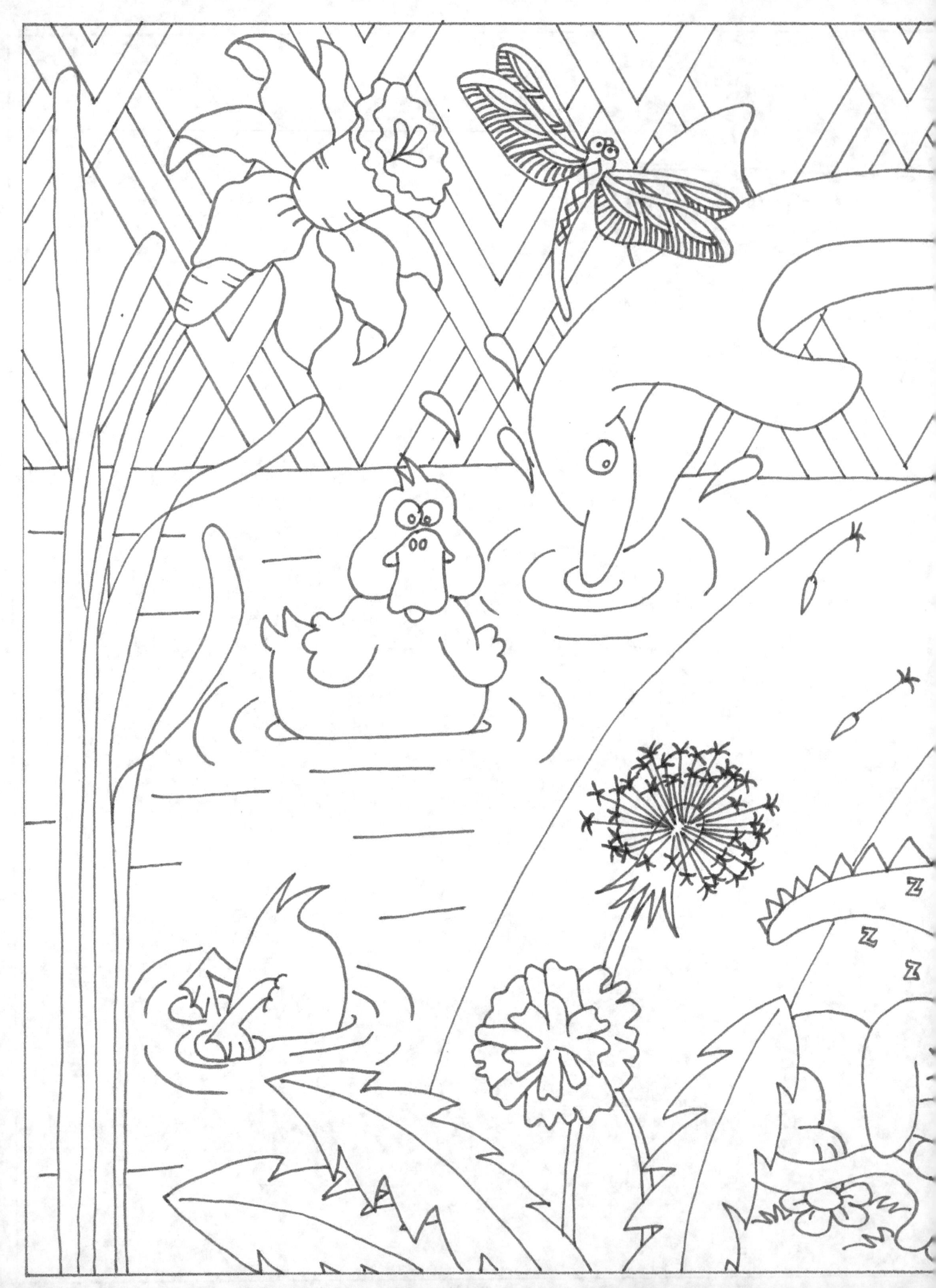

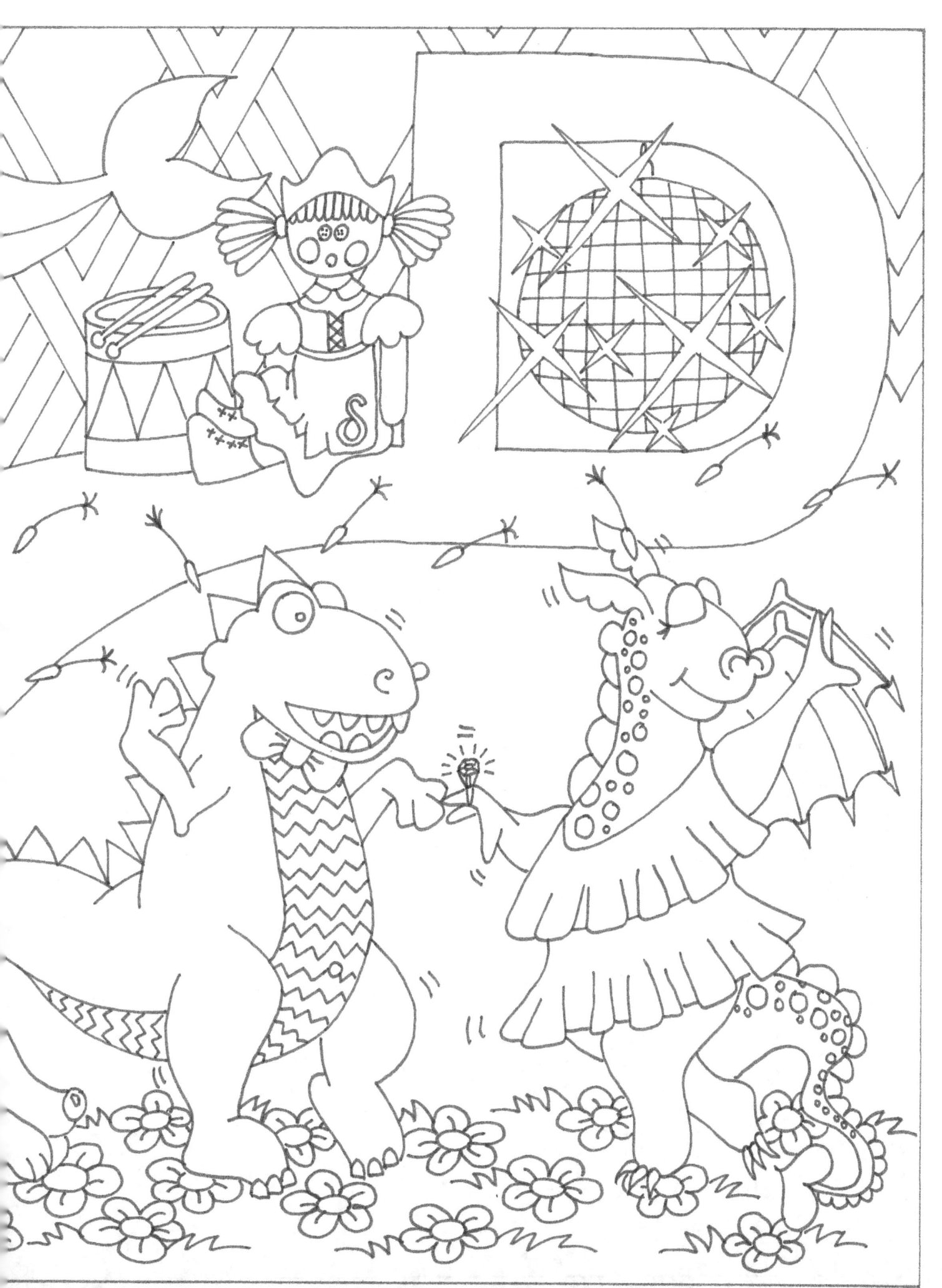

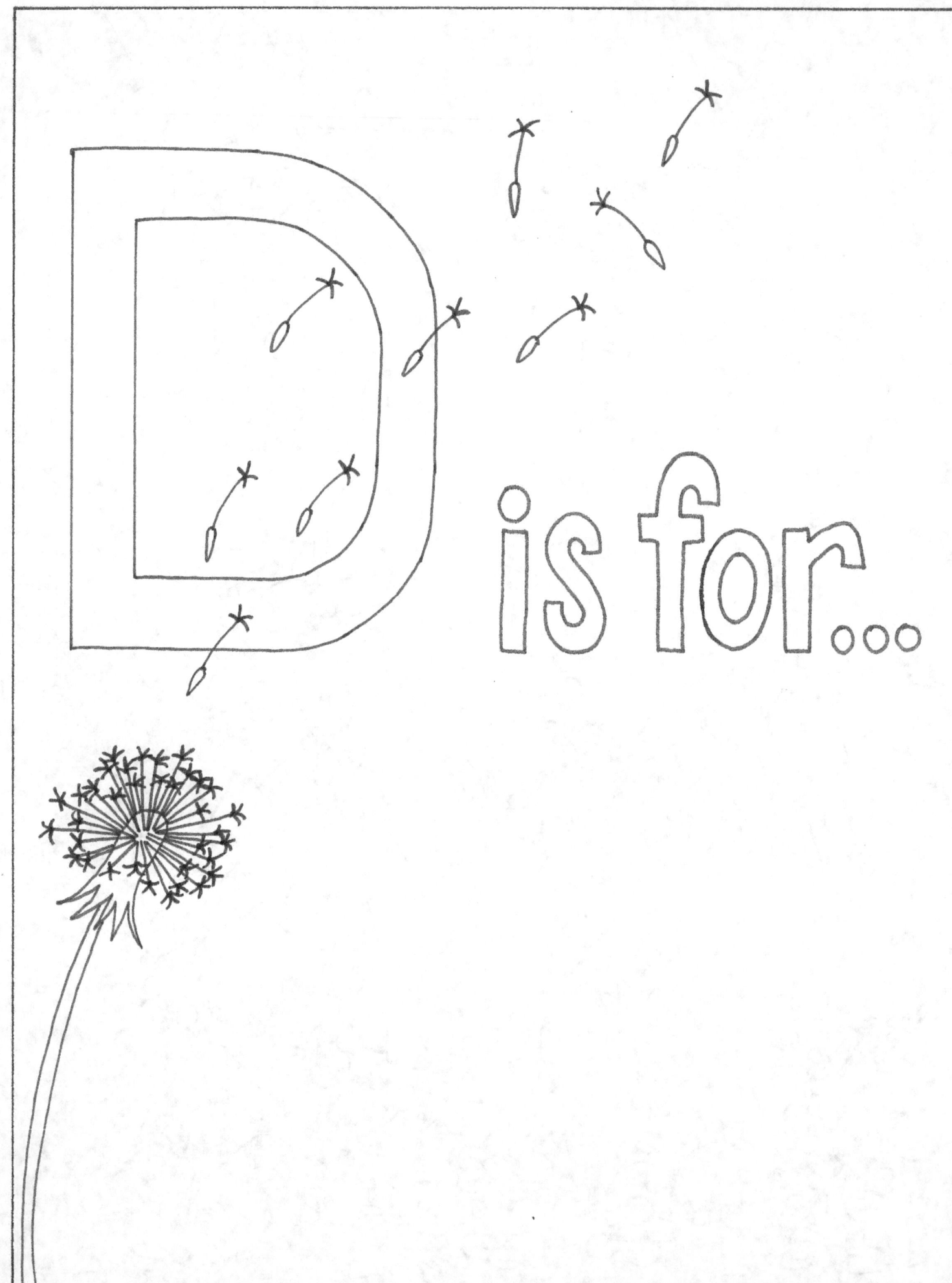

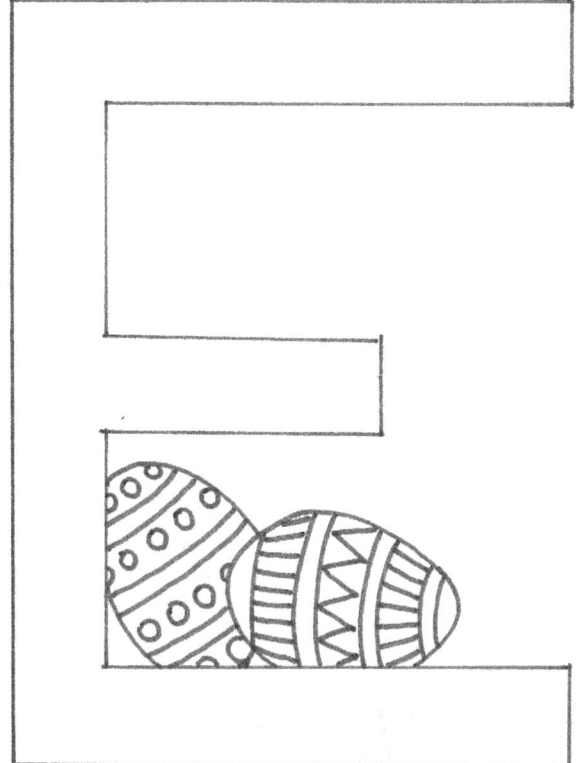

E is for...

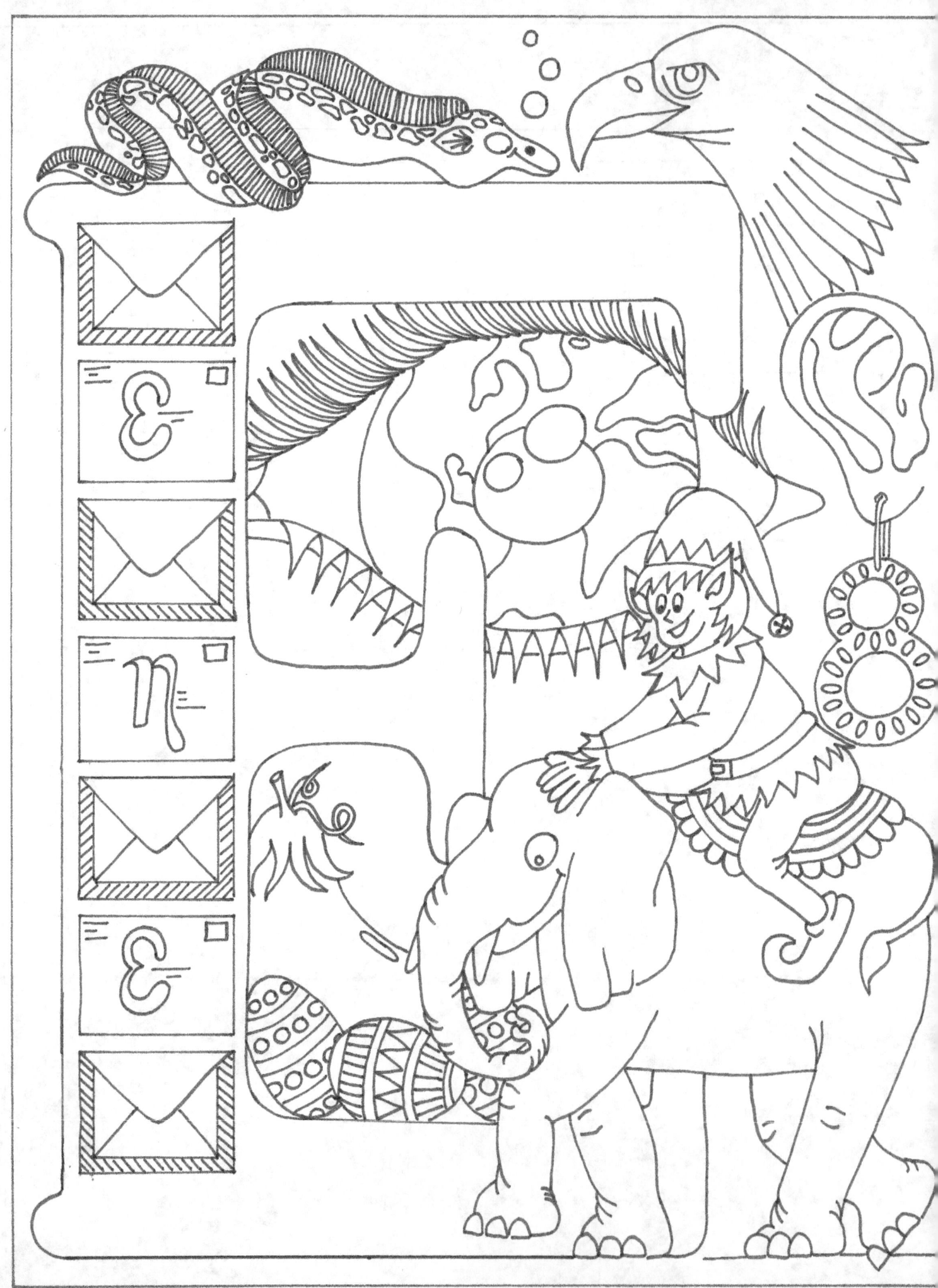

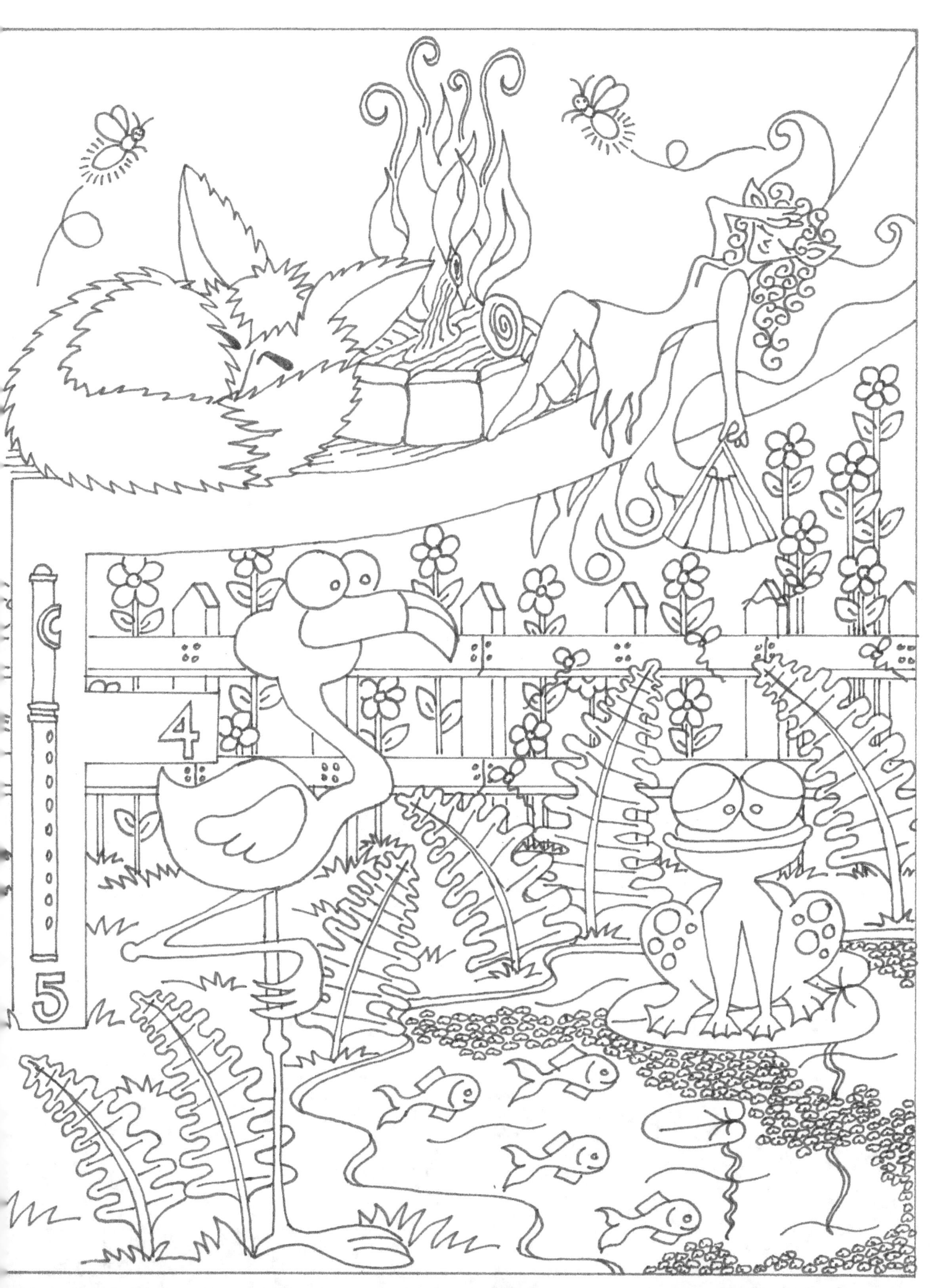

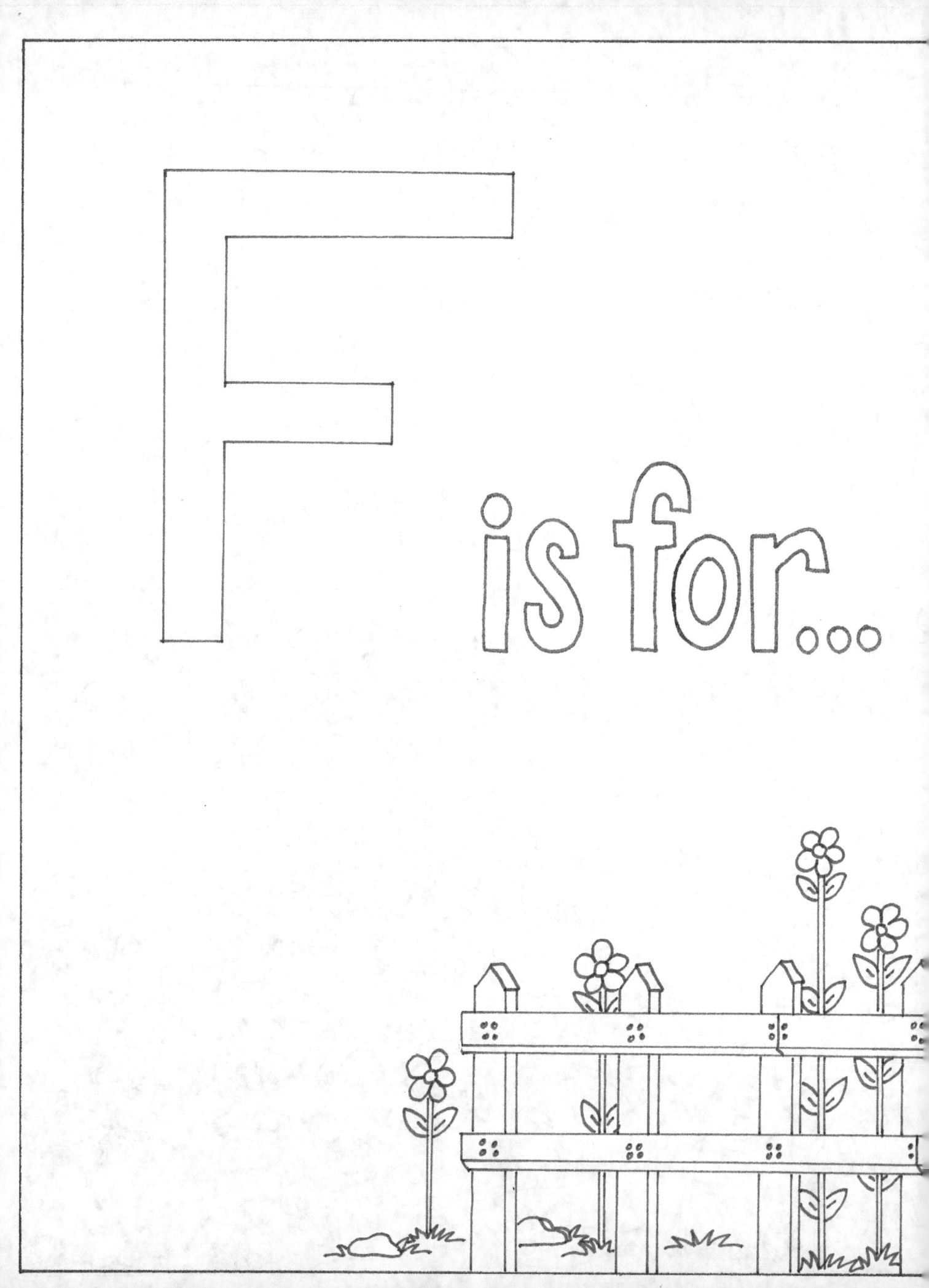

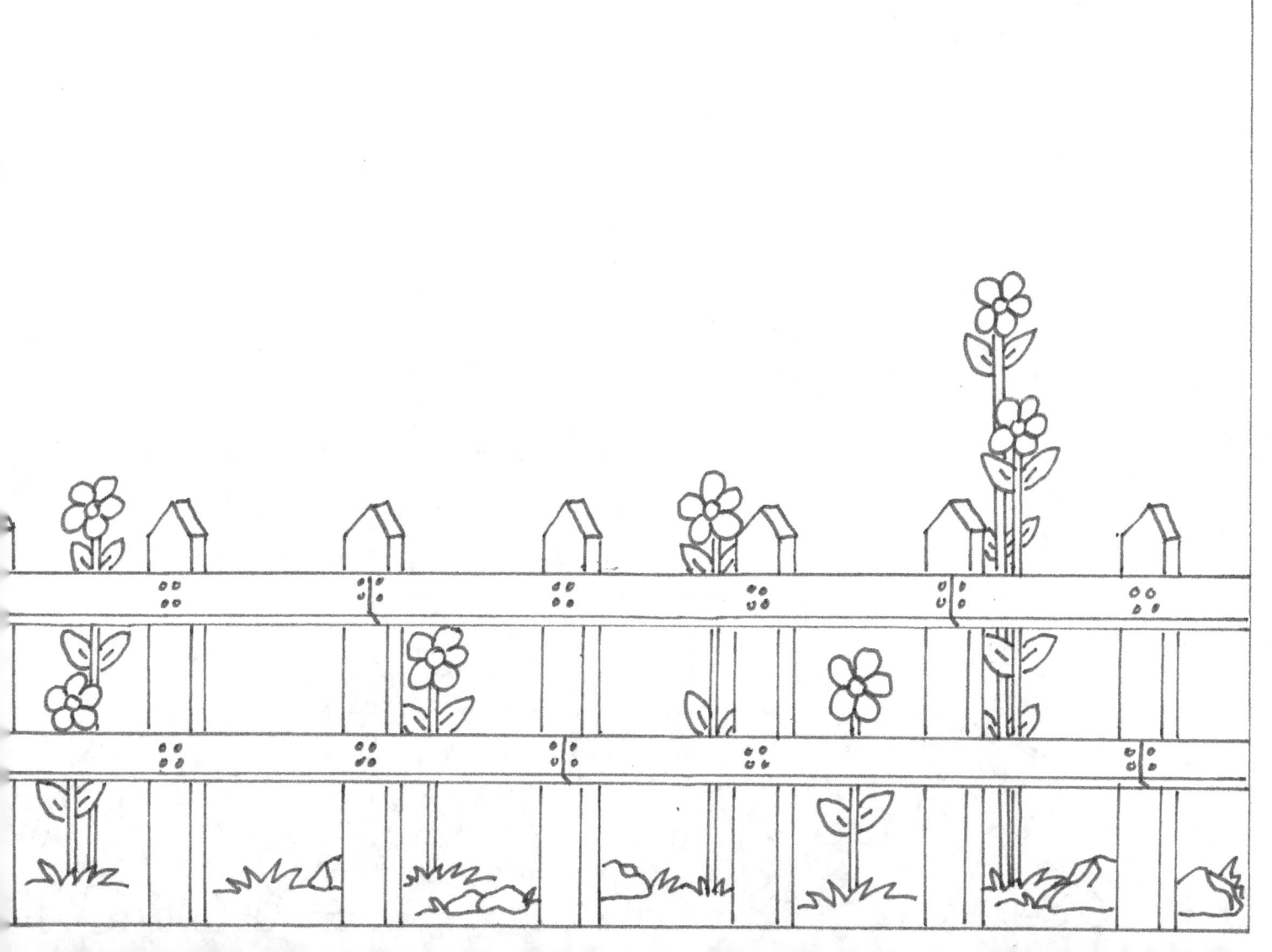

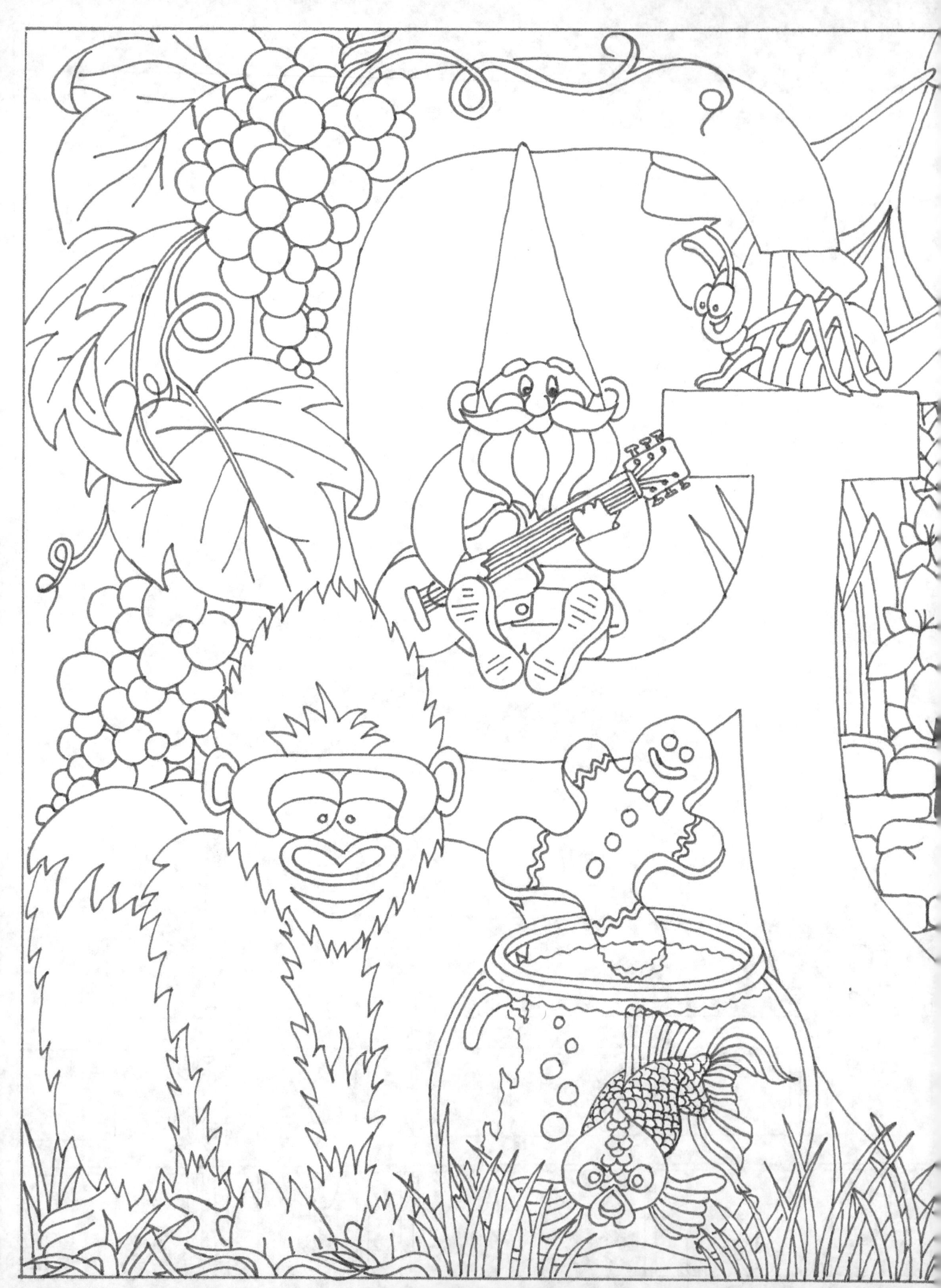

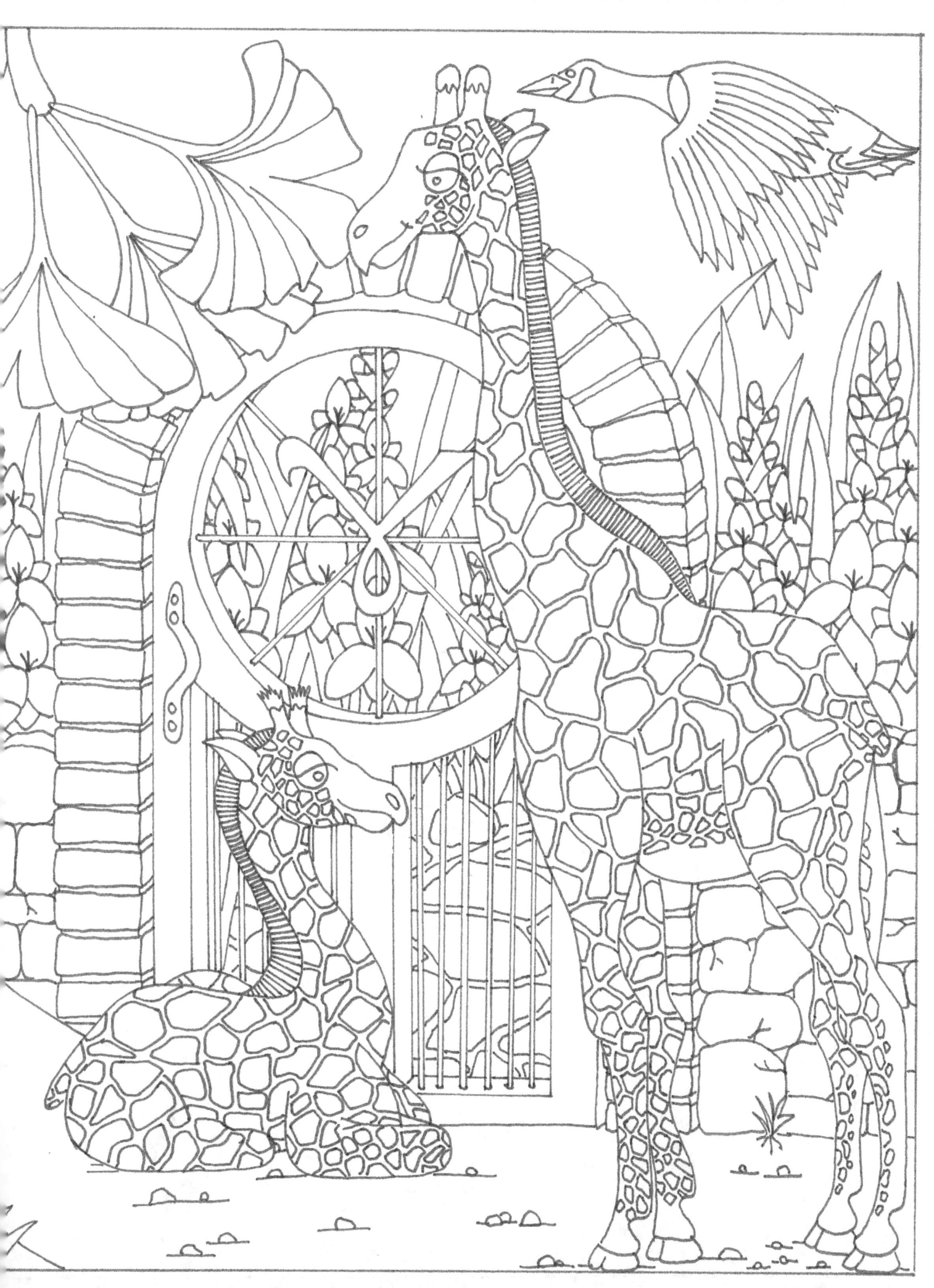

G is for...

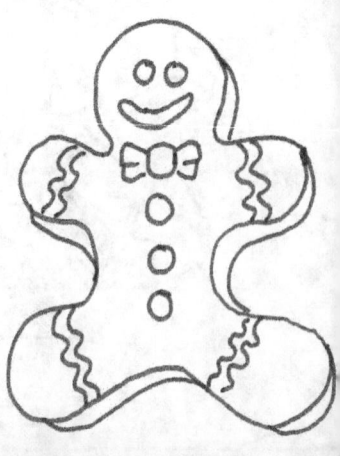

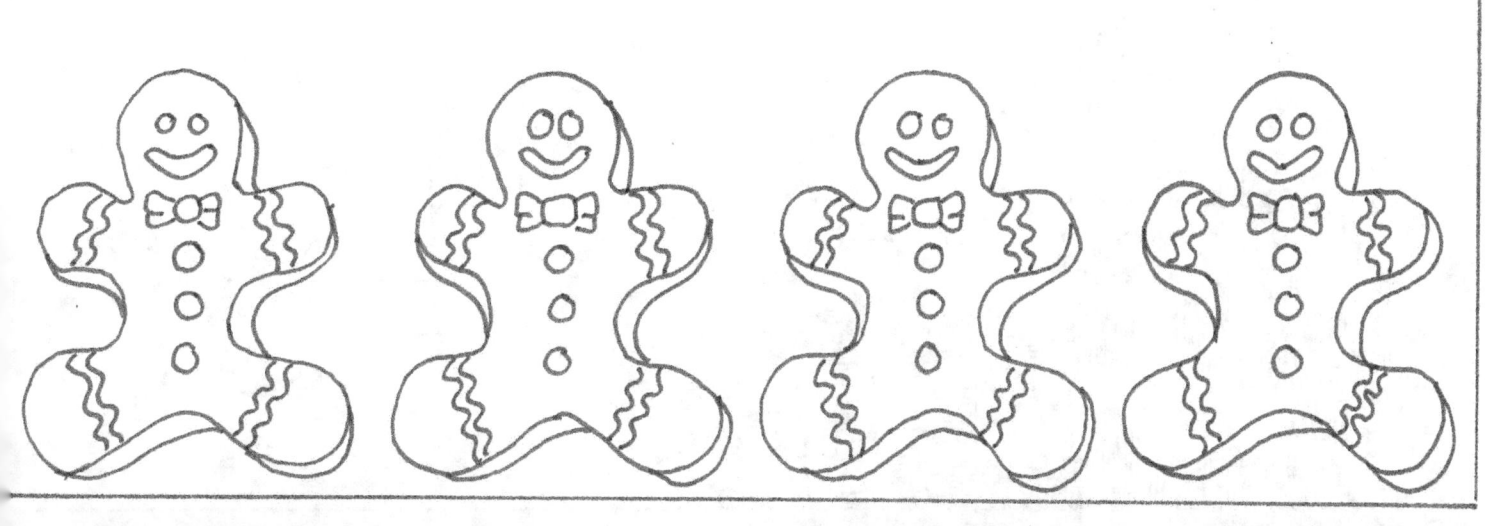

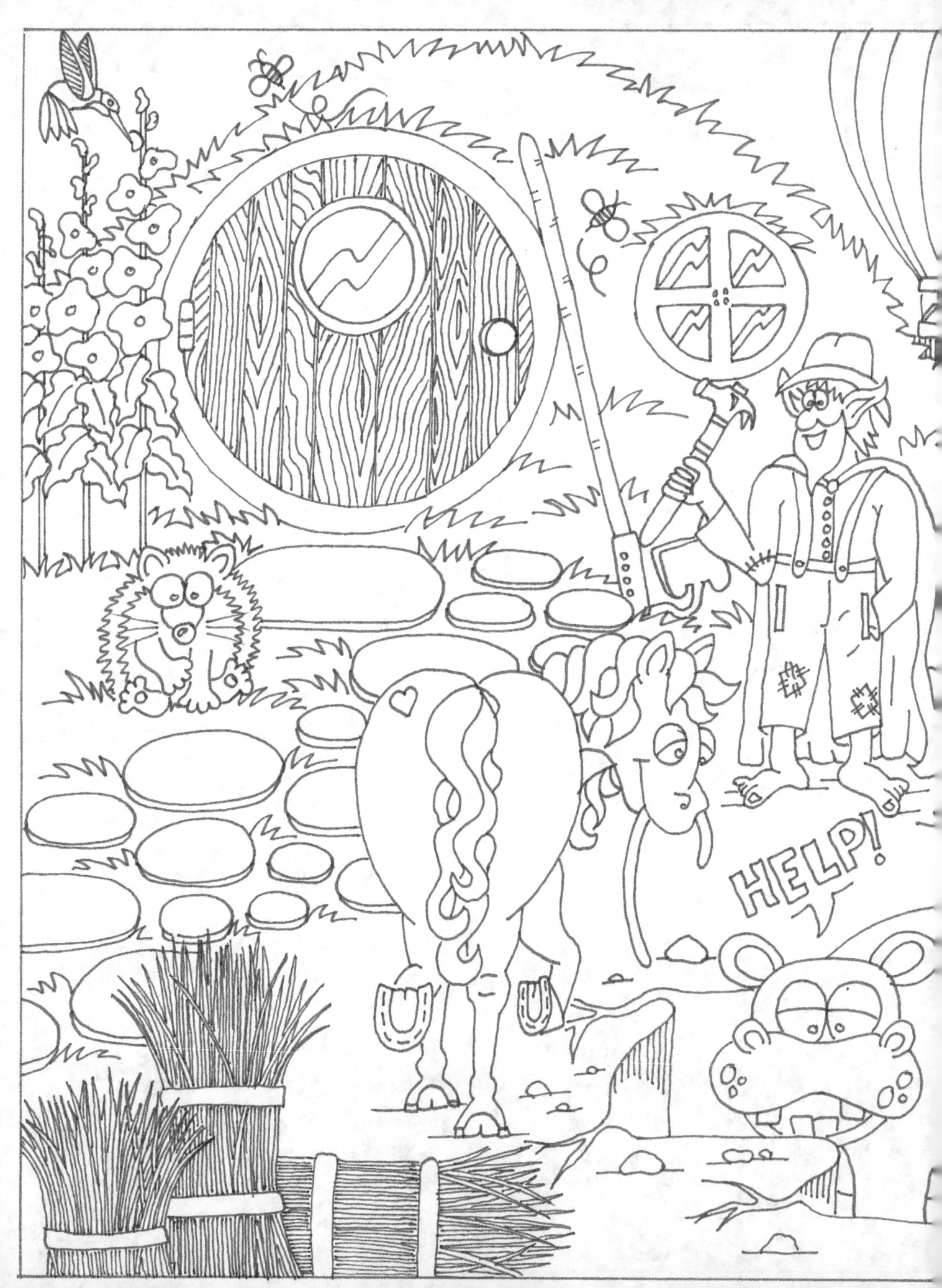

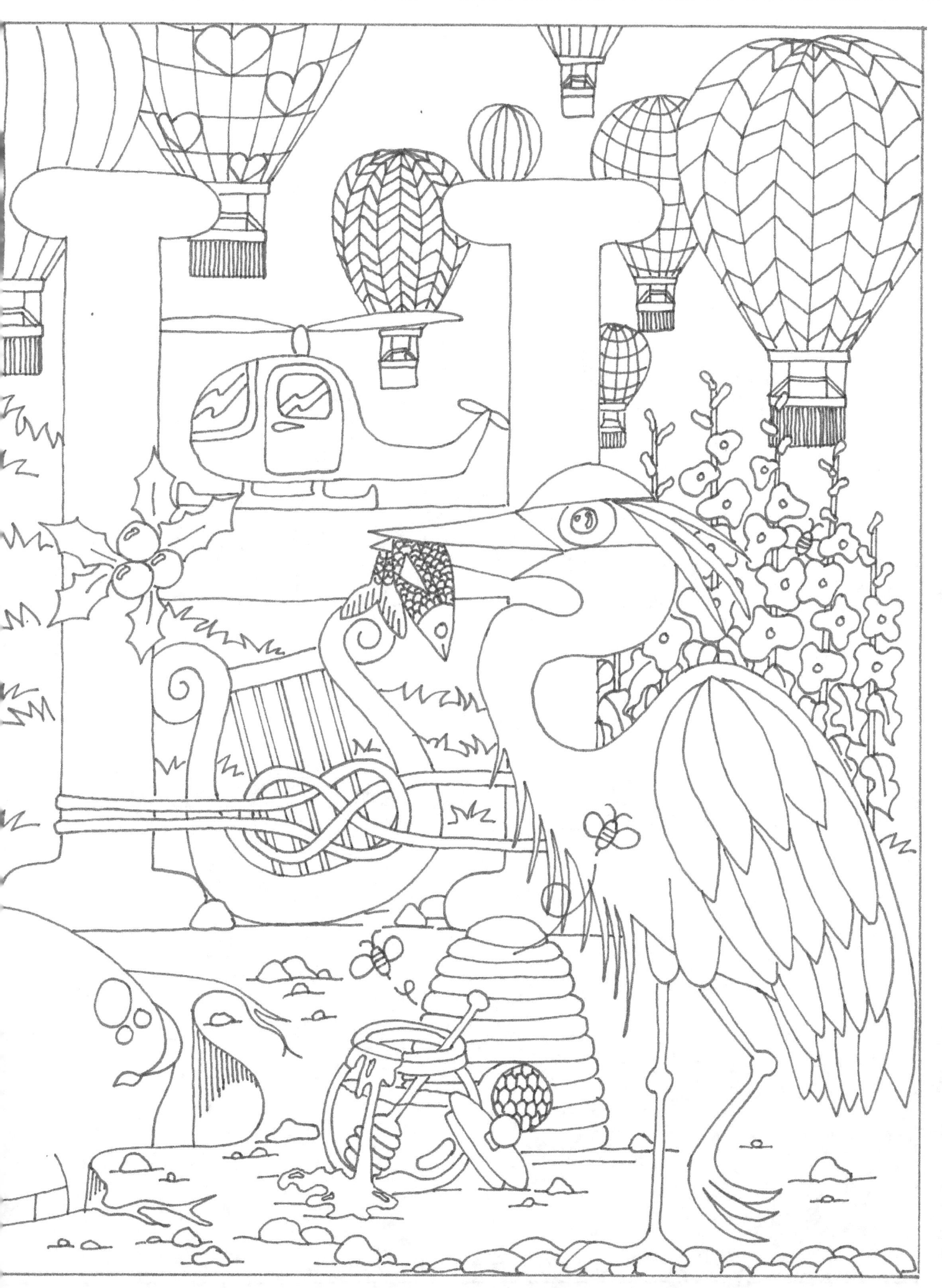

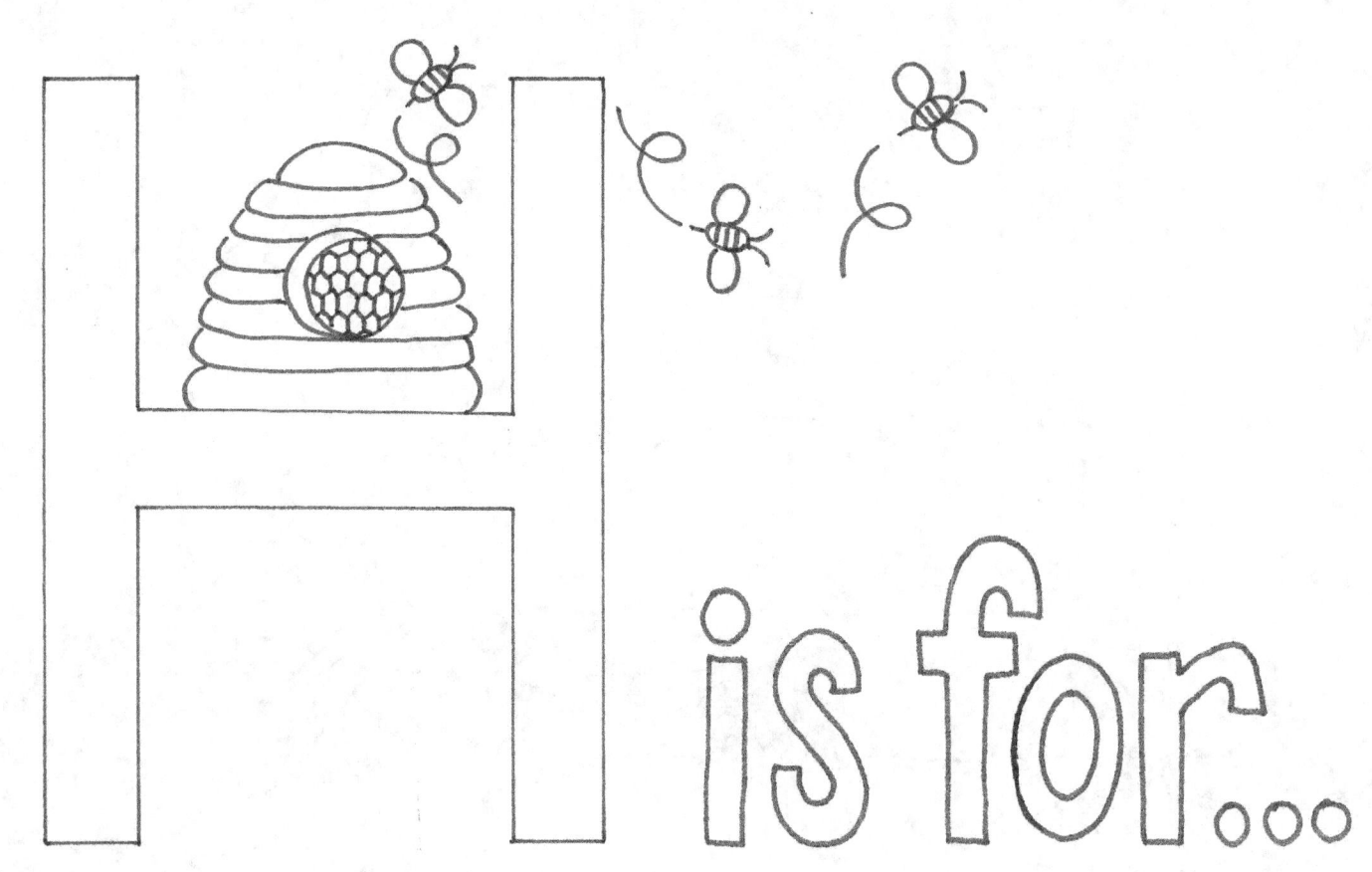

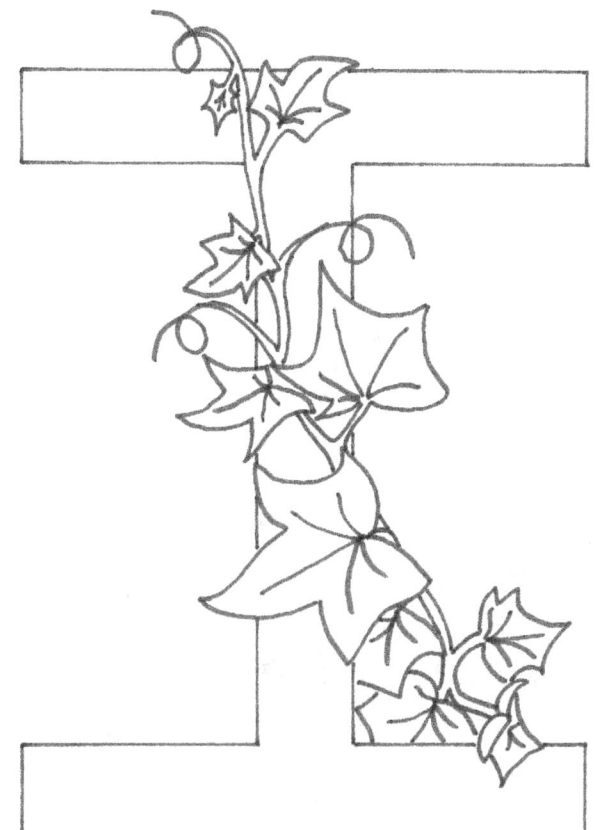 is for...

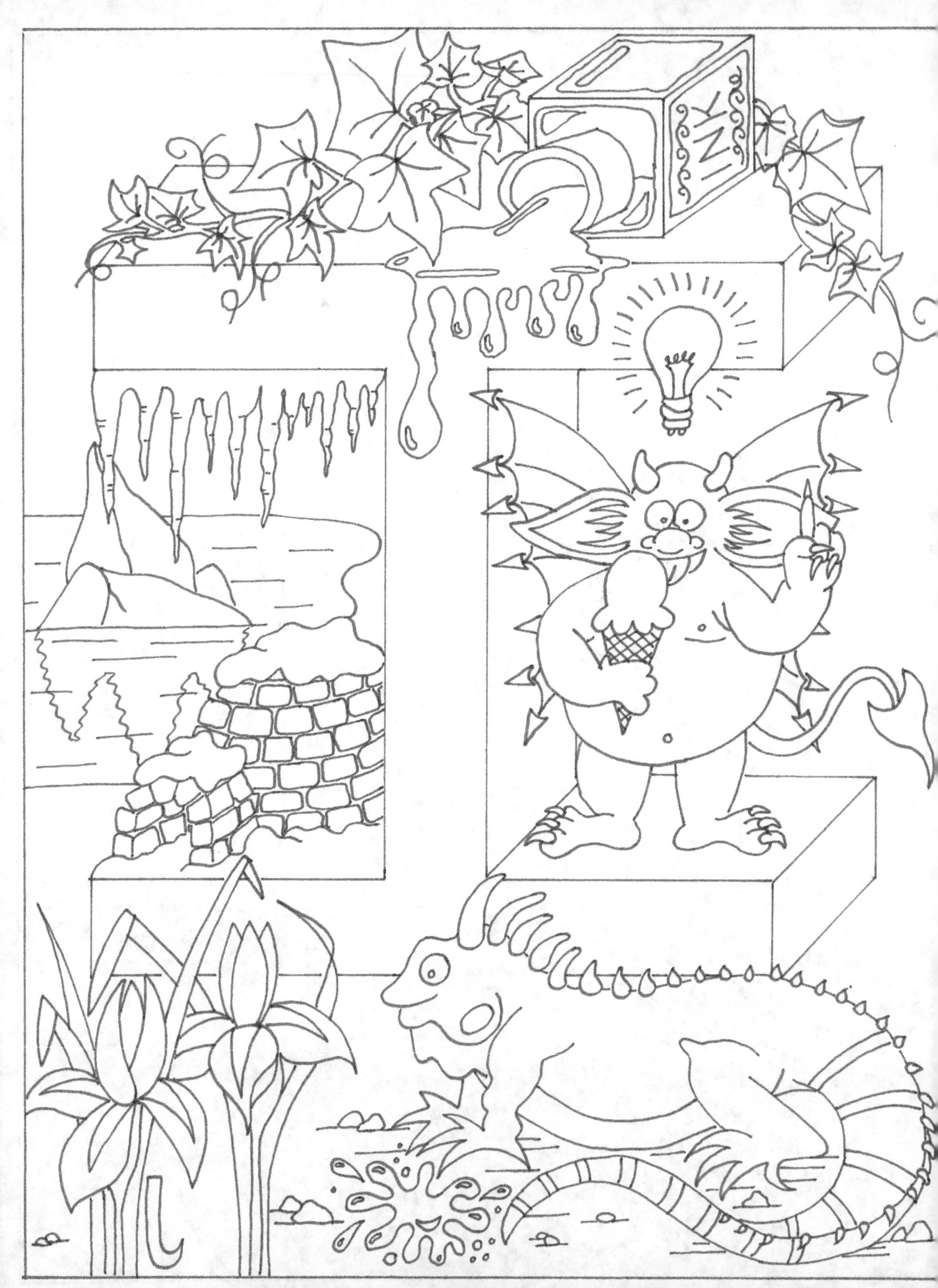

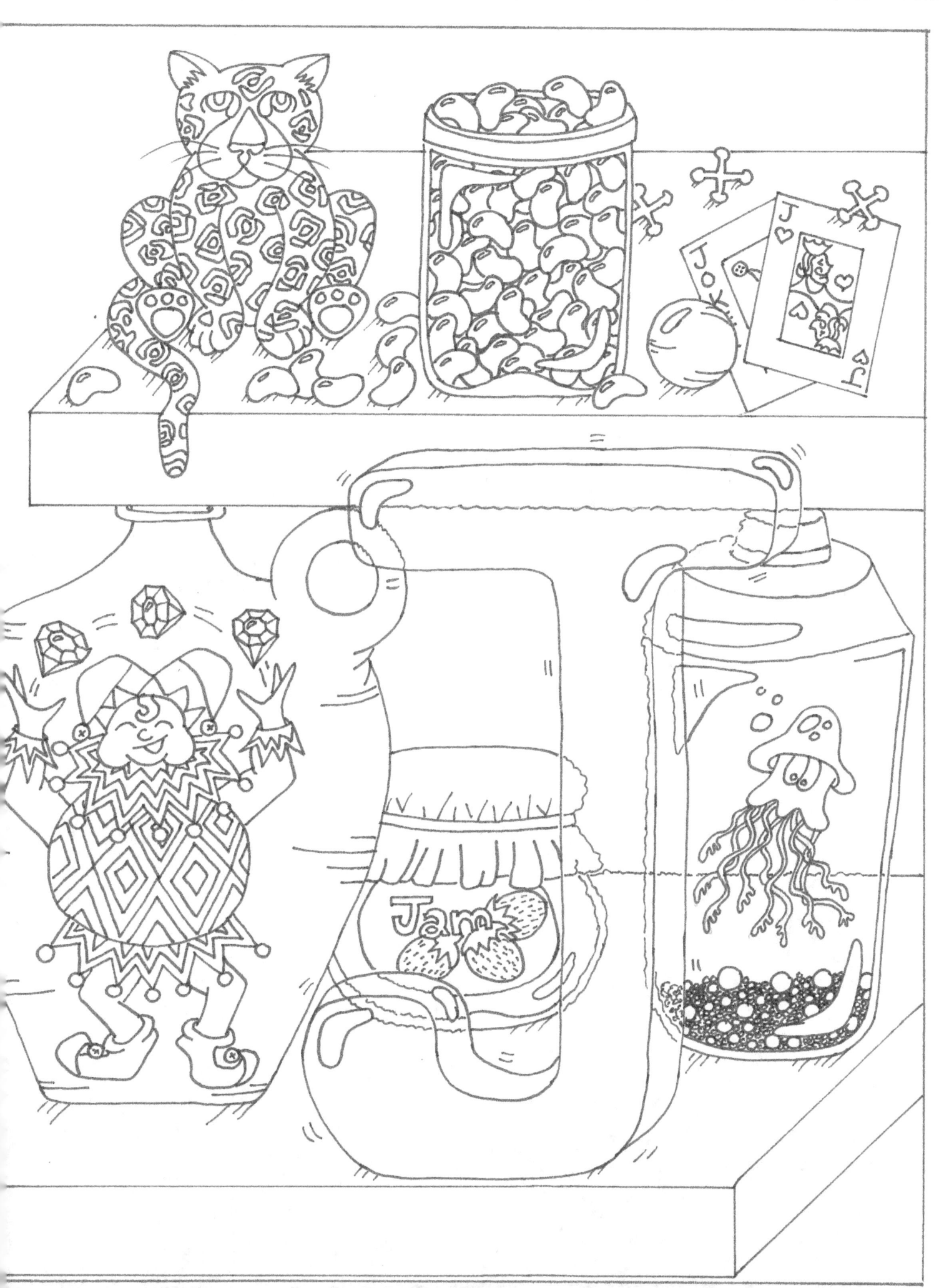

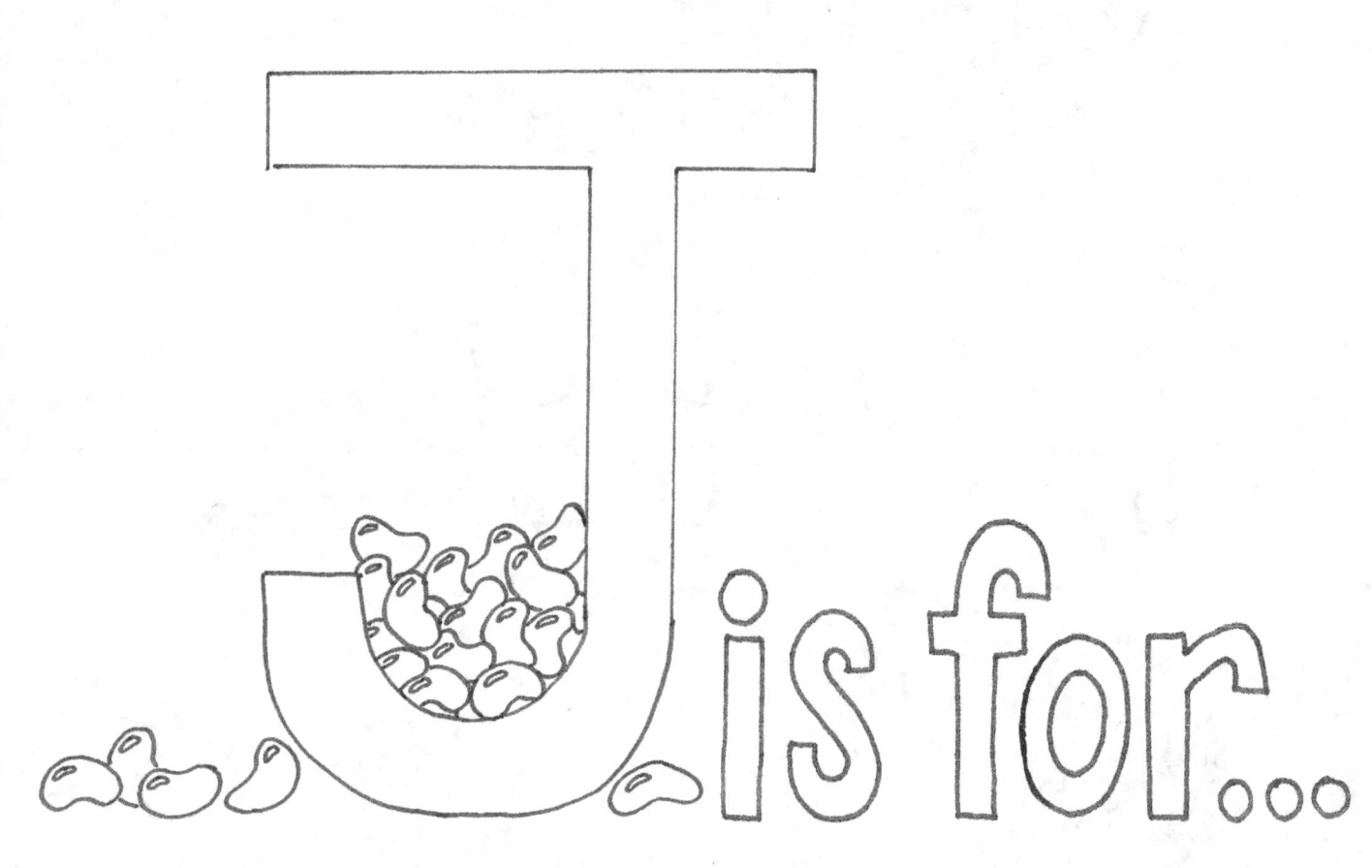

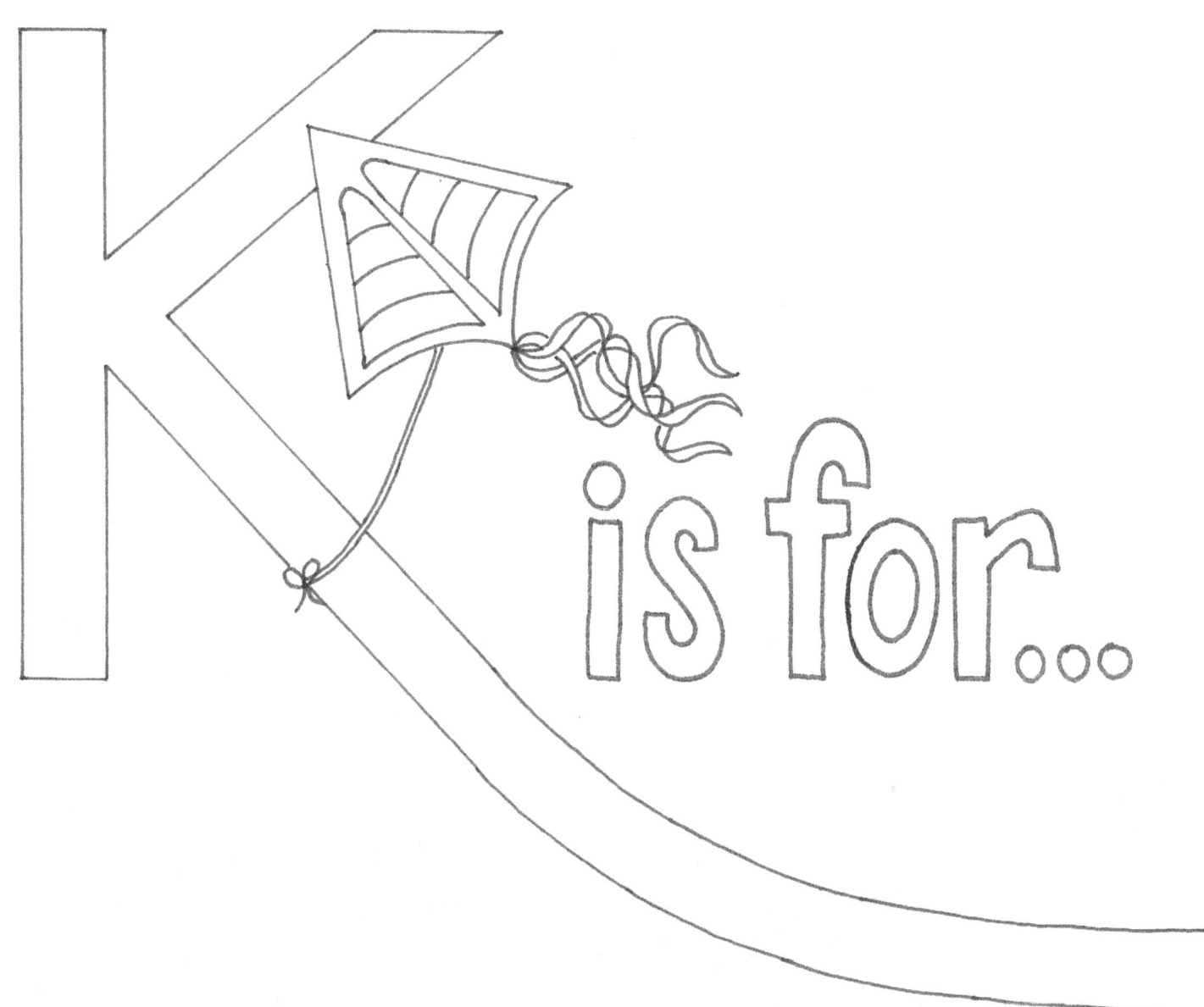

is for...

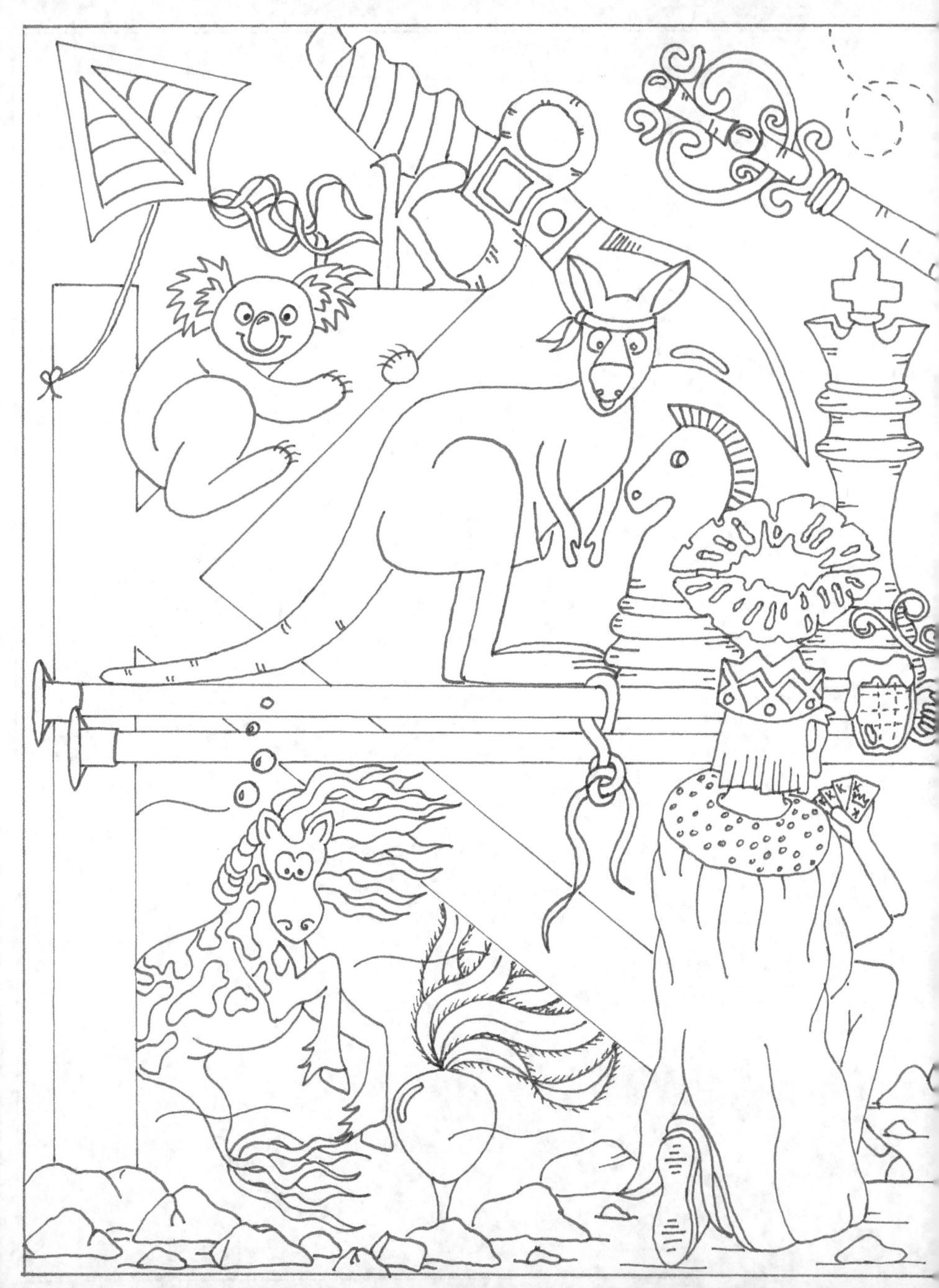

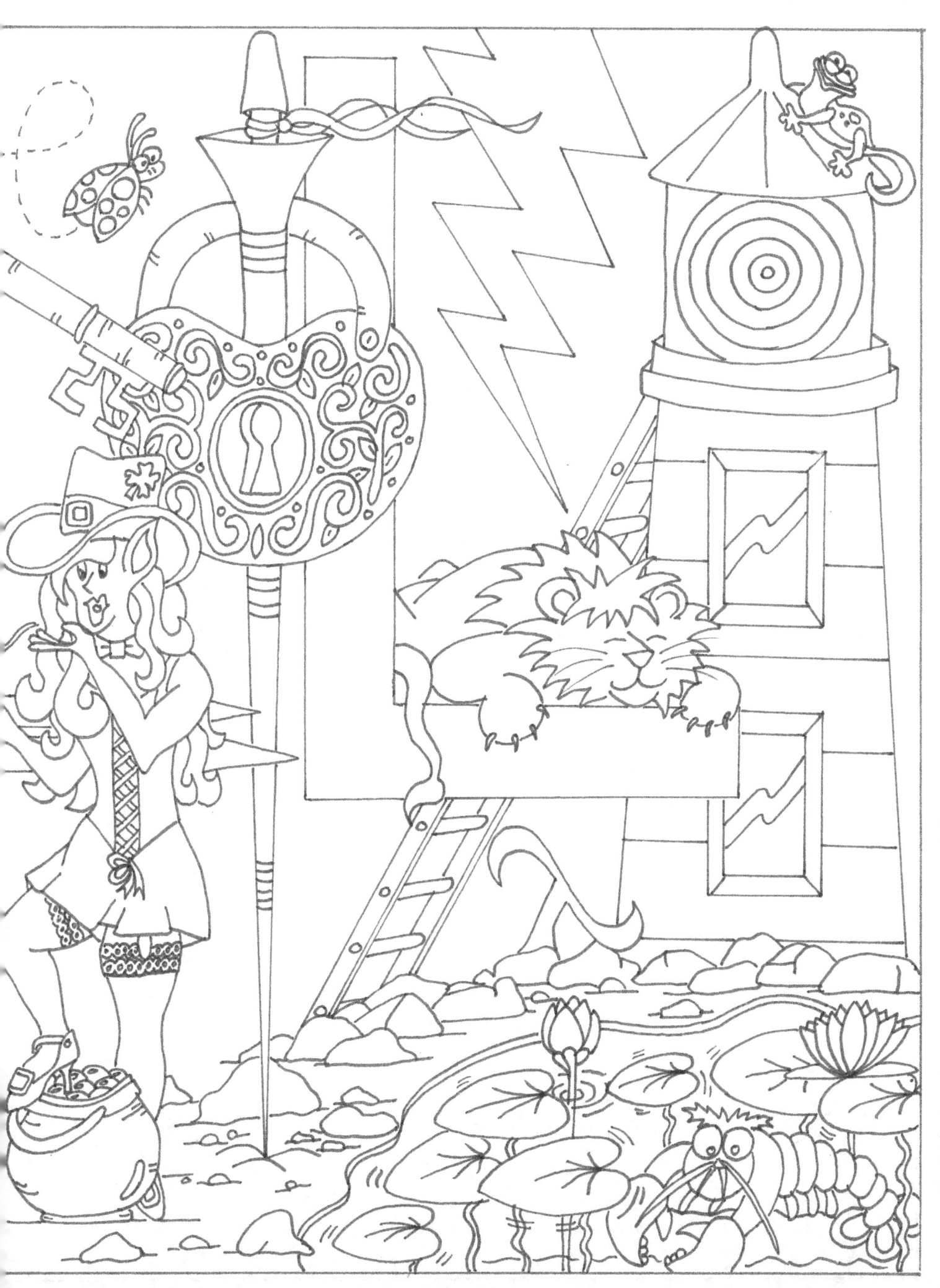

L is for...

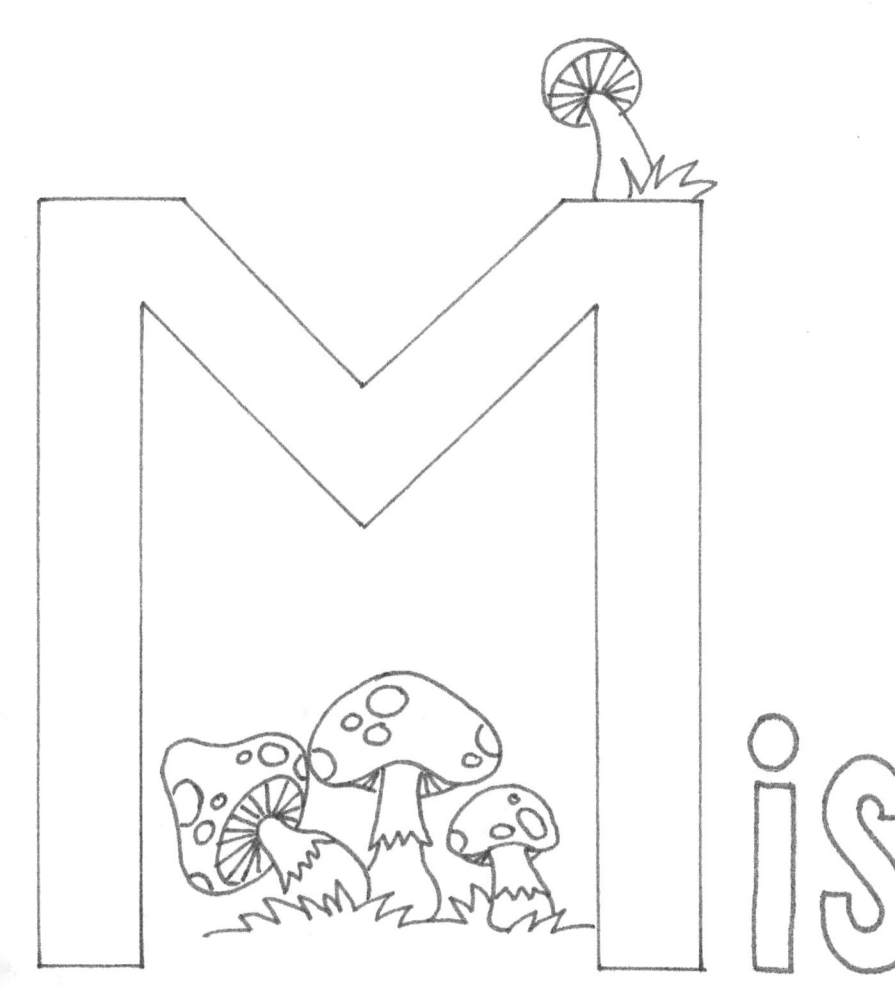 is for...

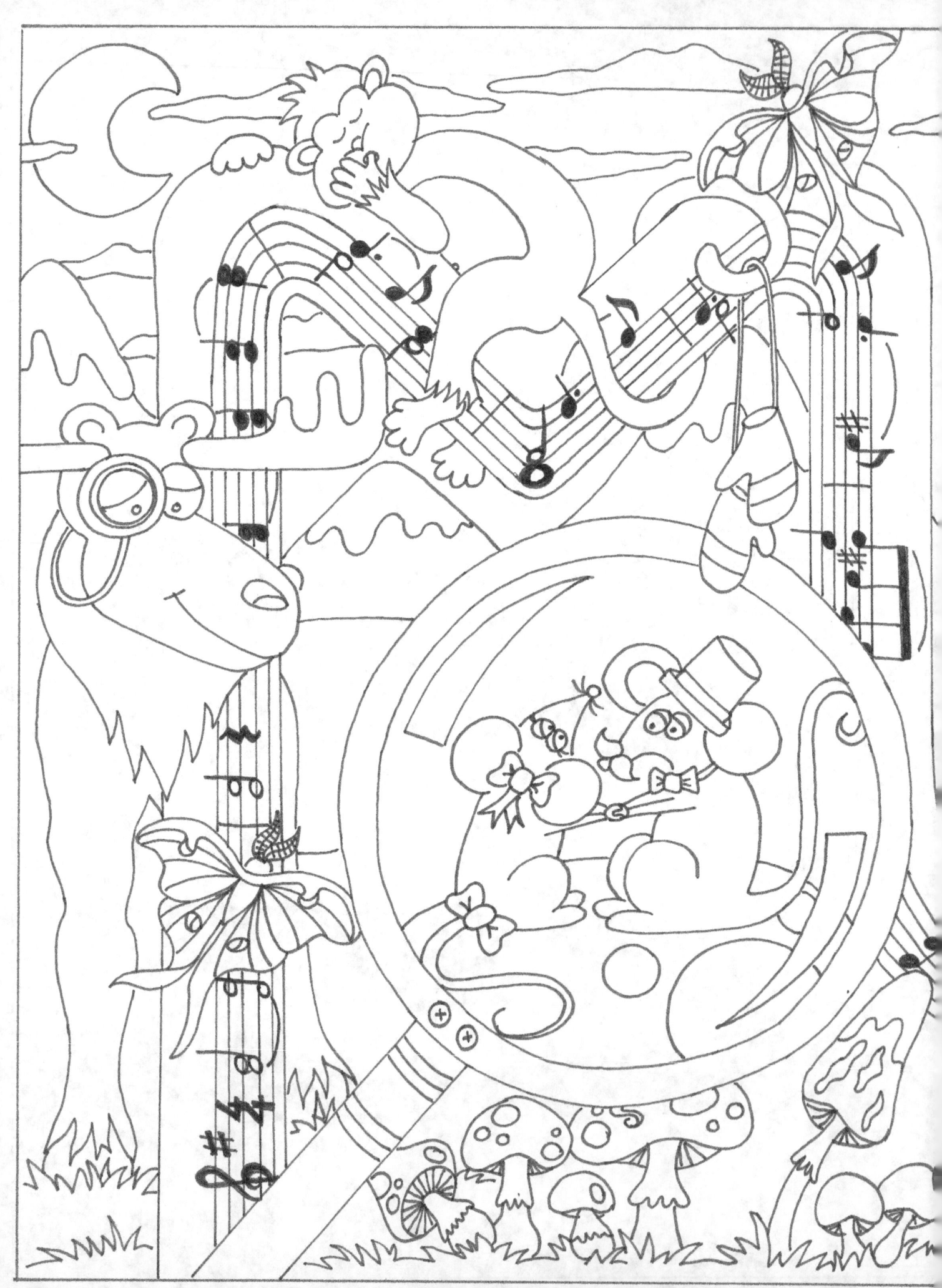

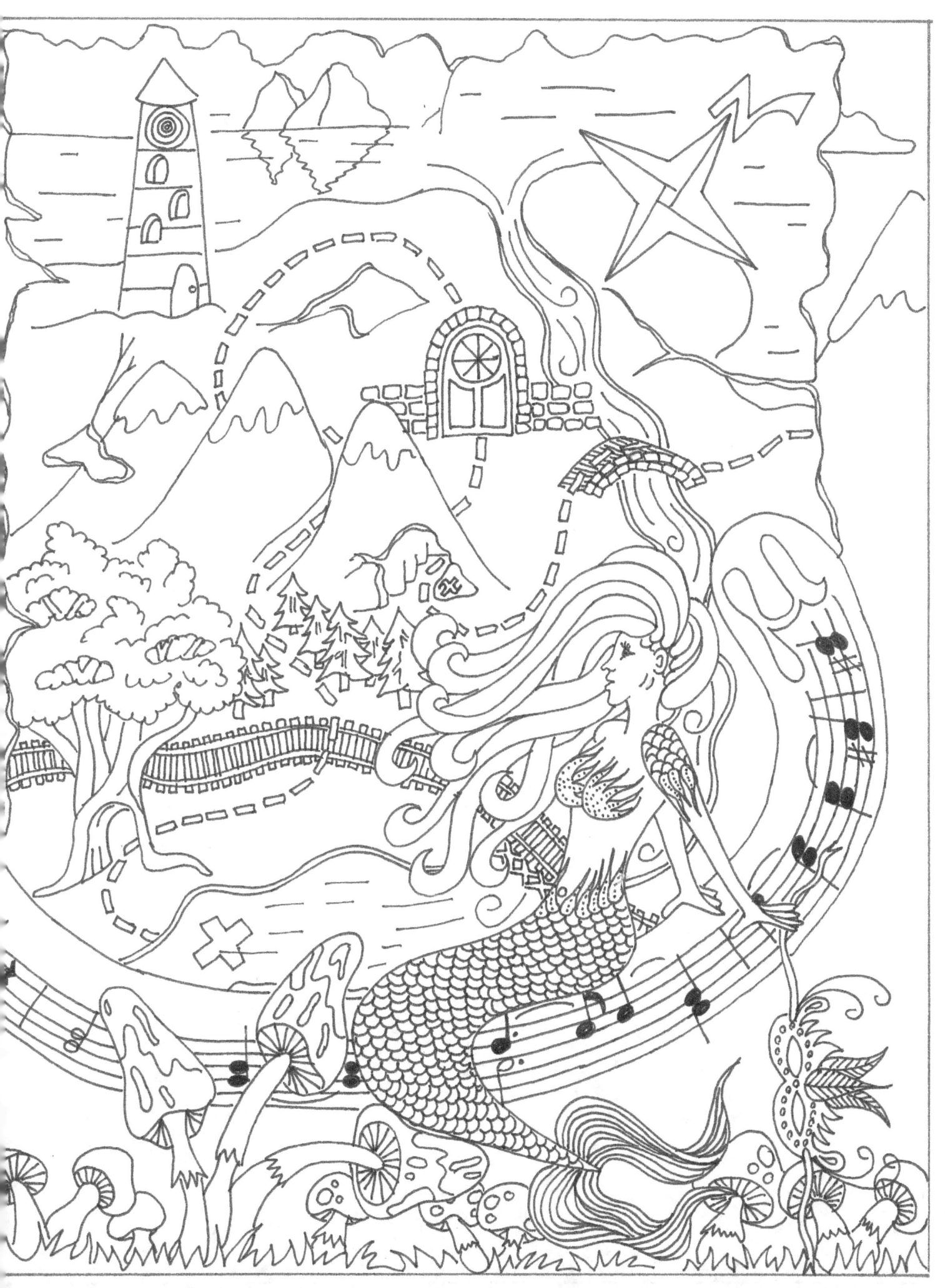

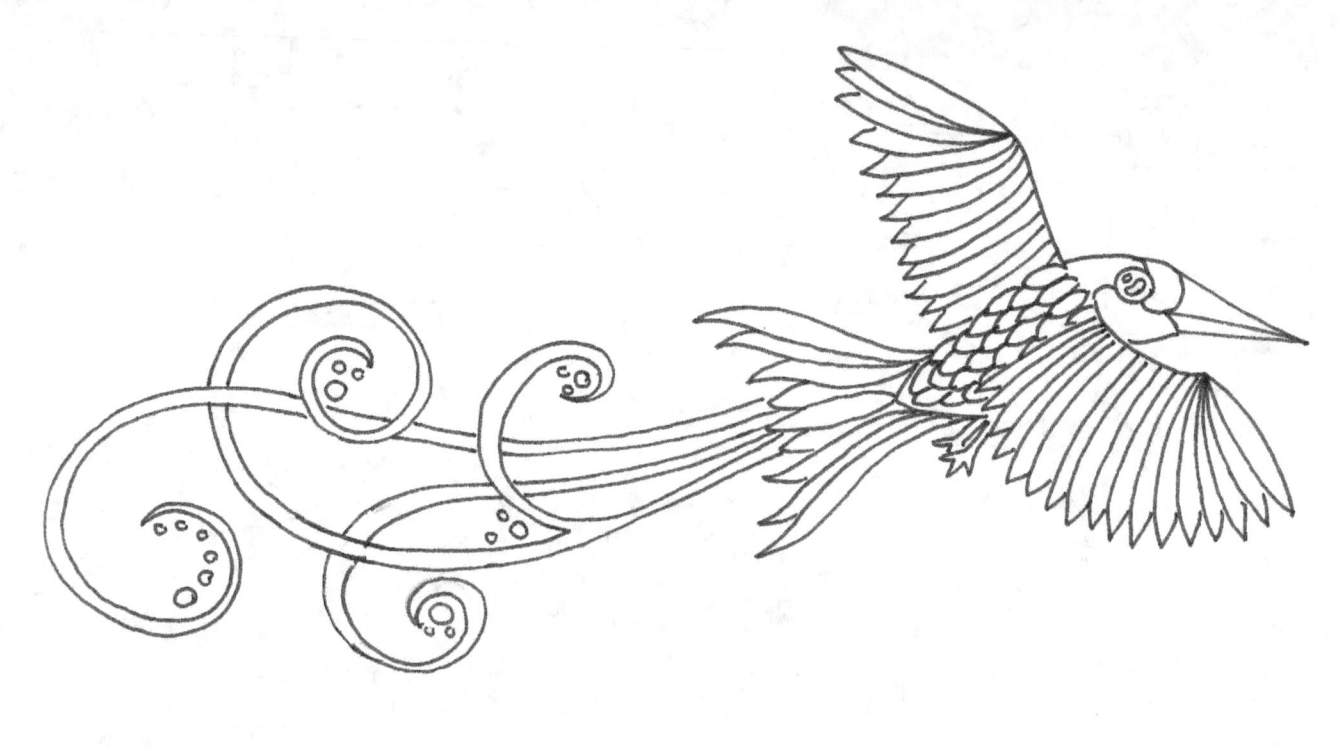

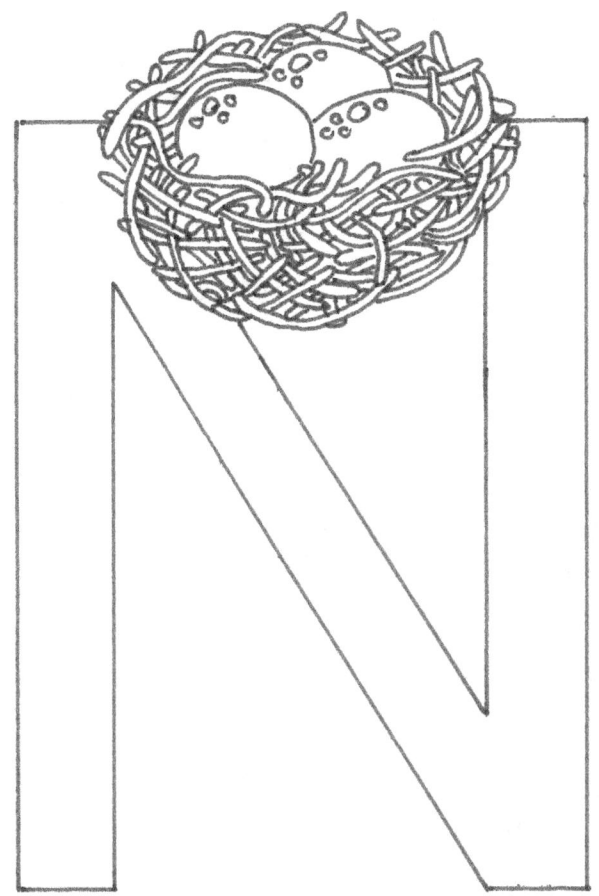

N is for...

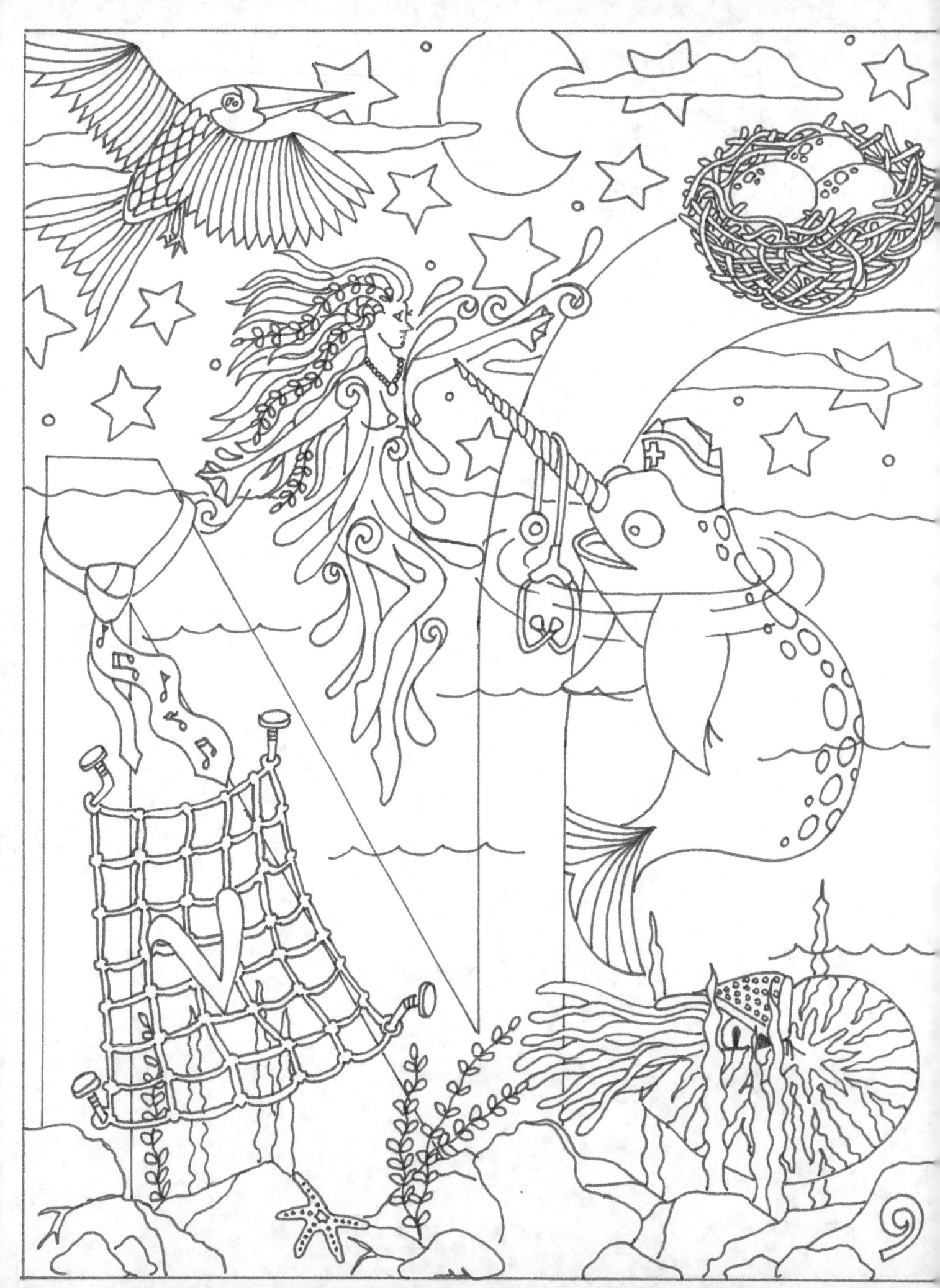

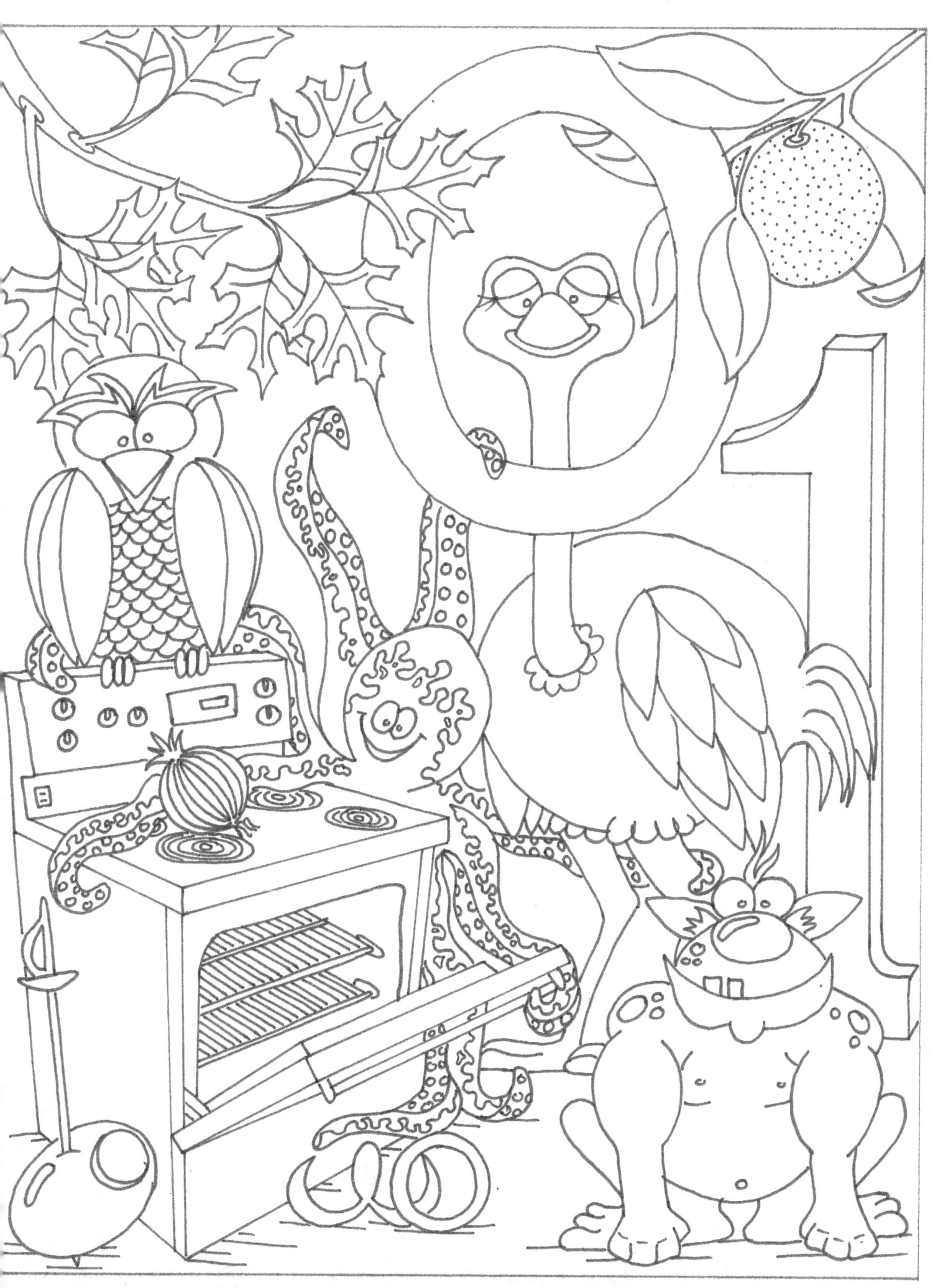

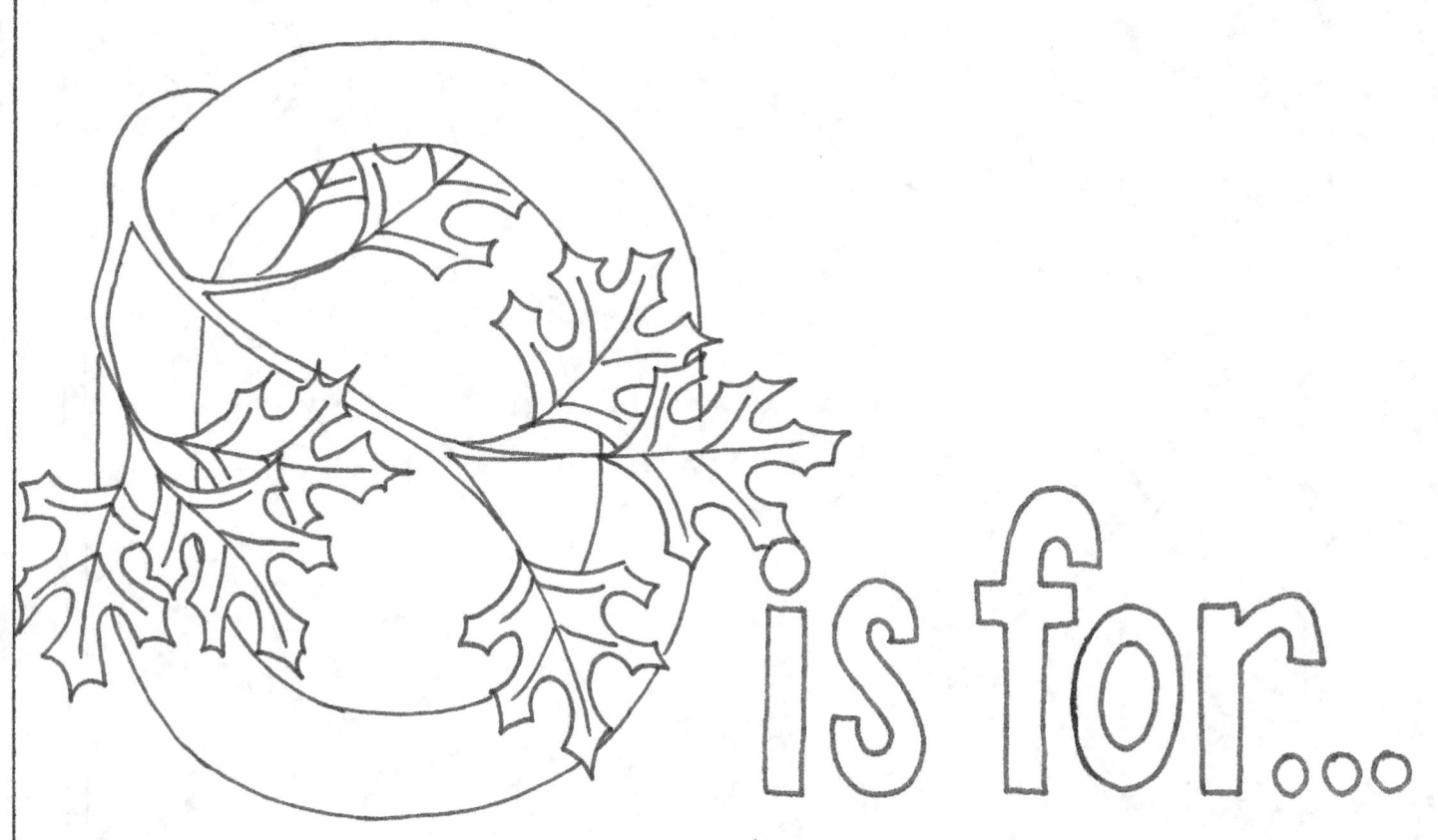

is for...

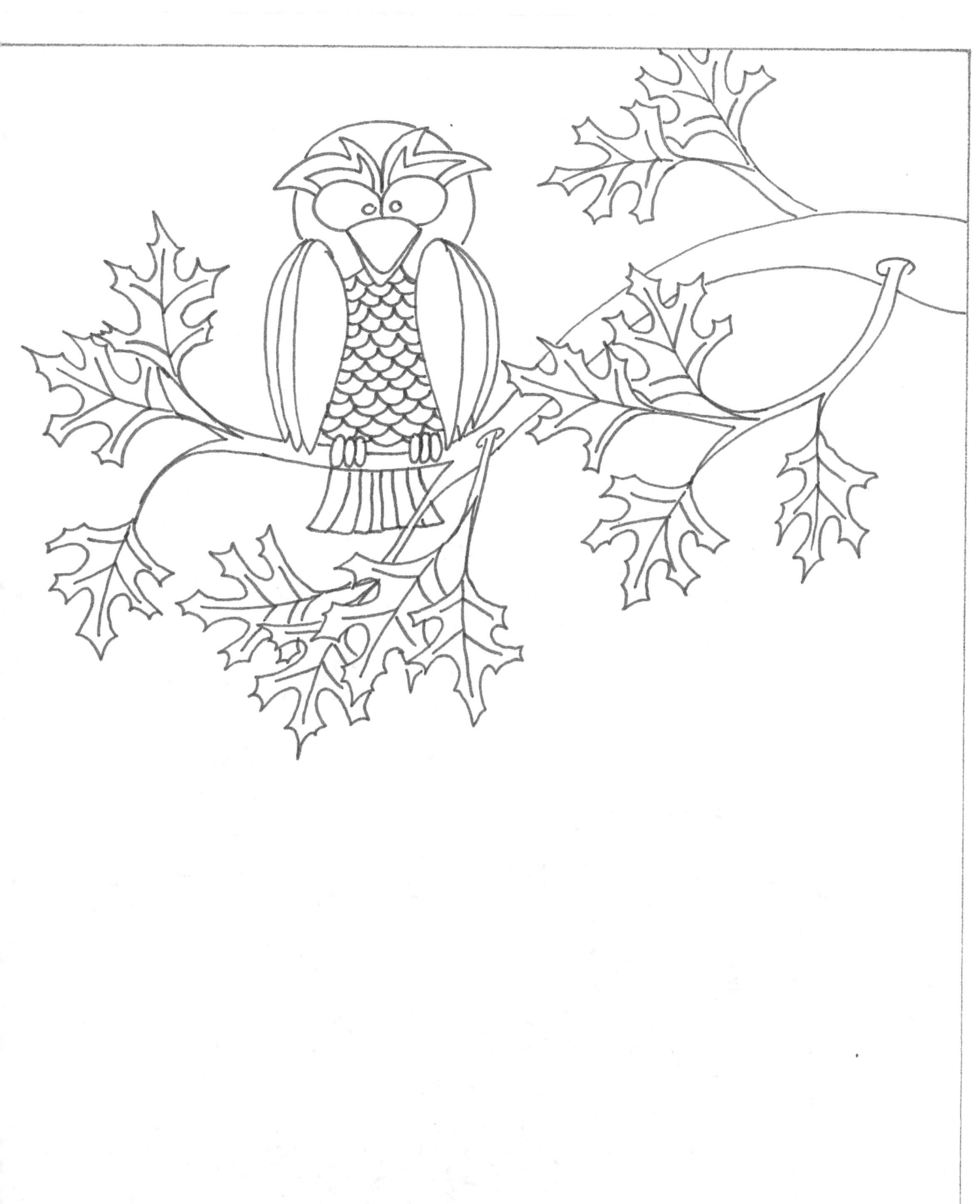

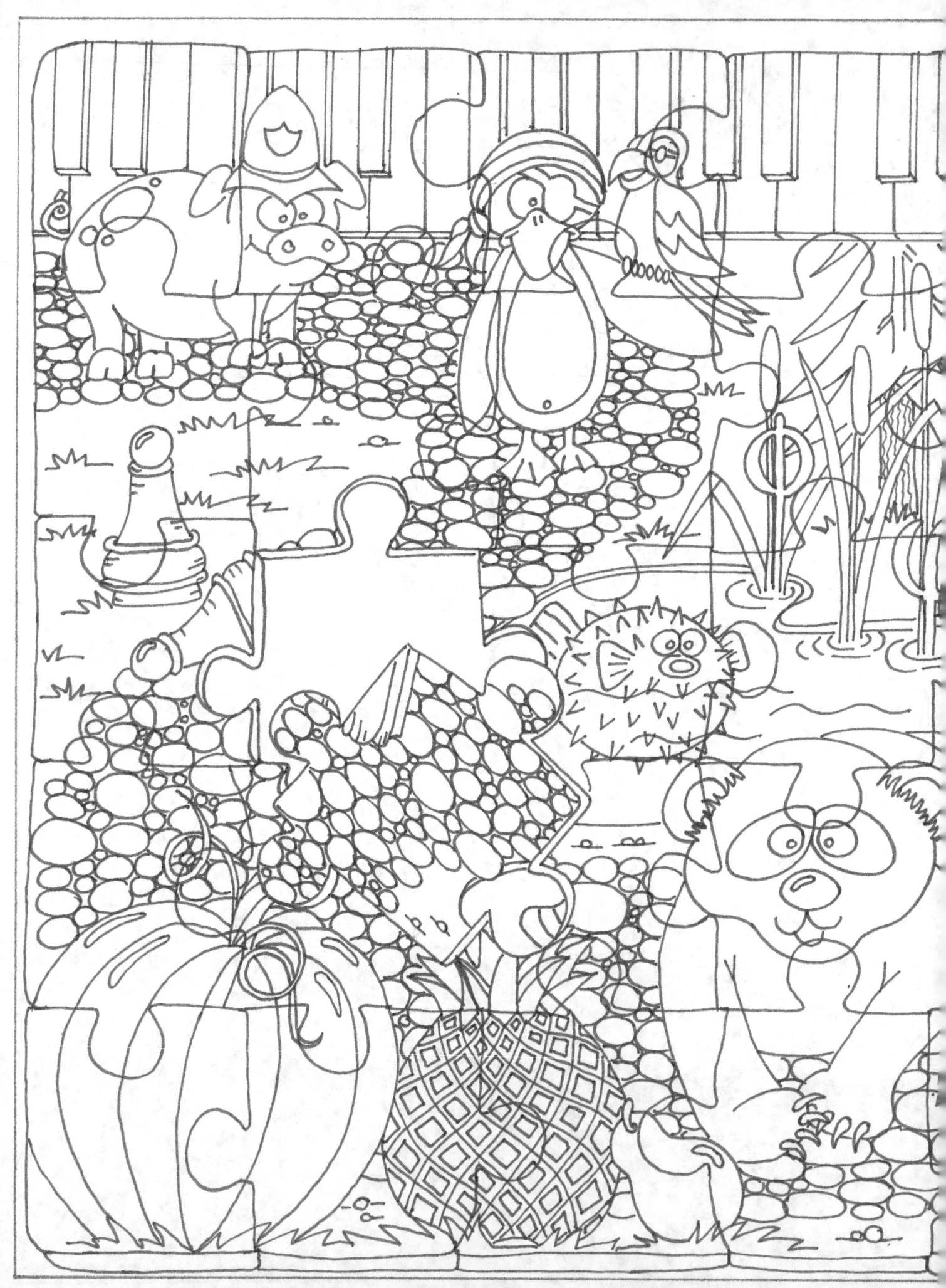

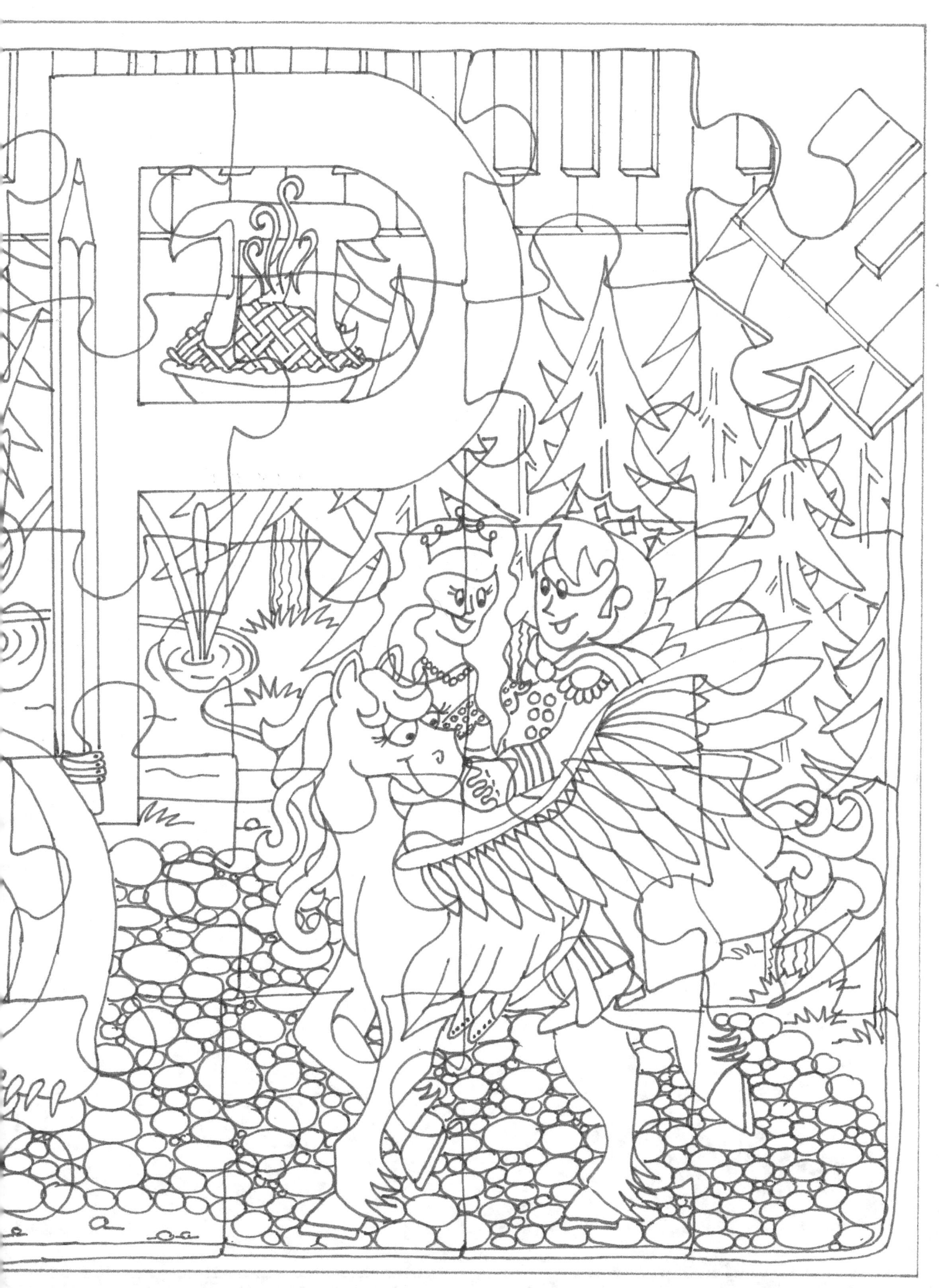

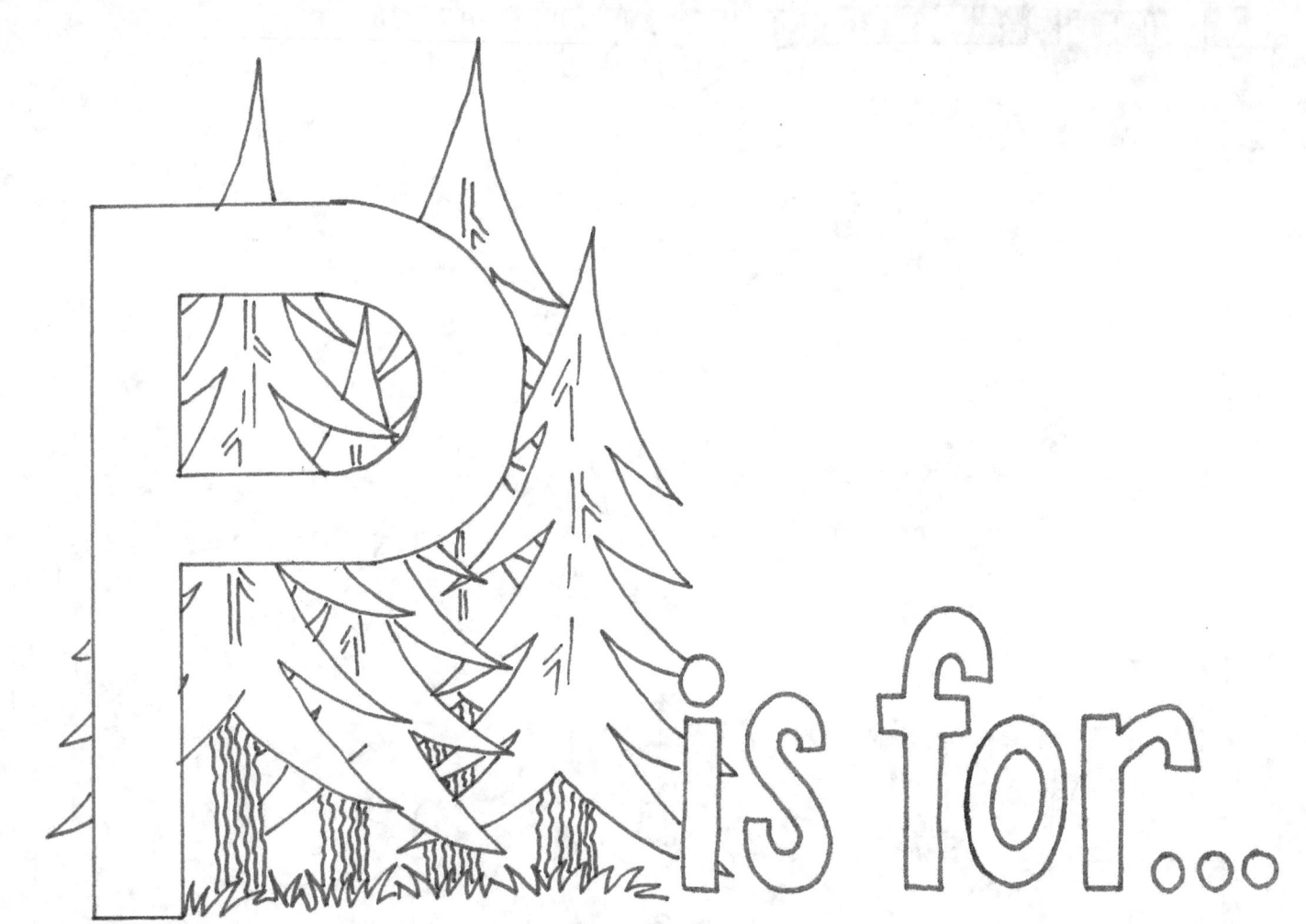

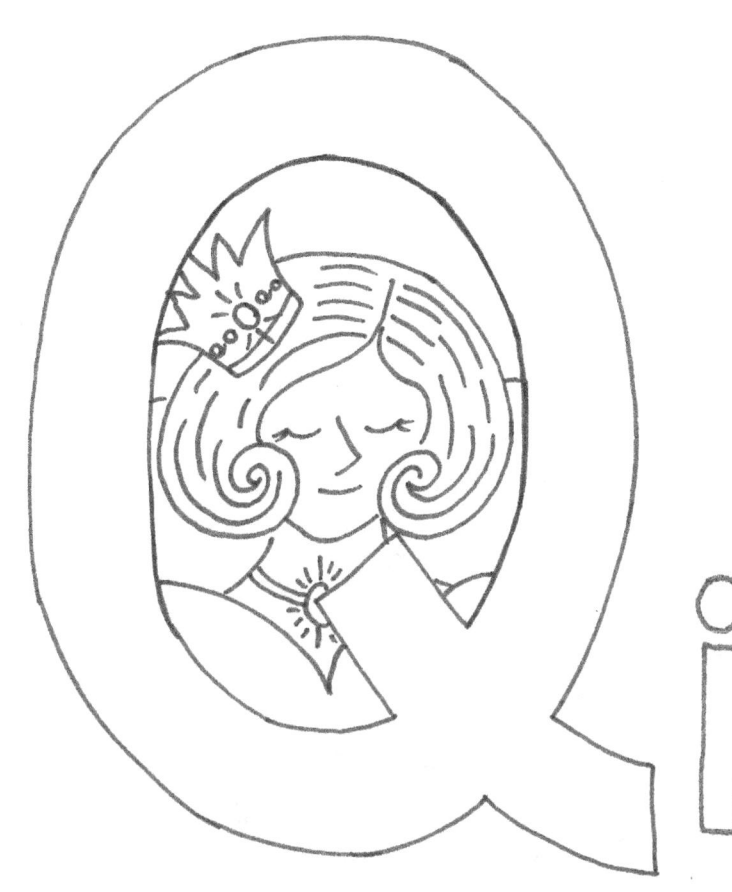 is for...

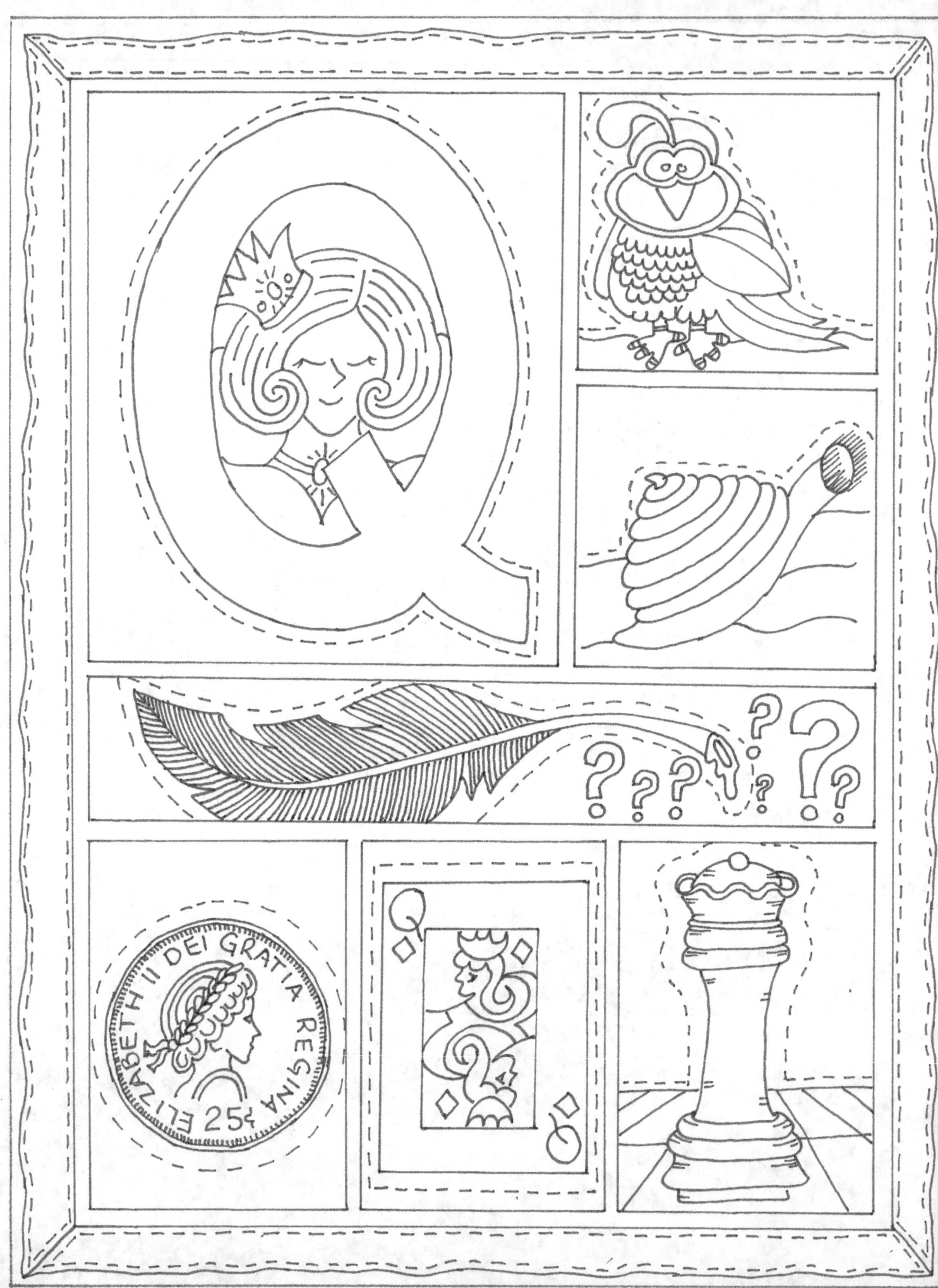

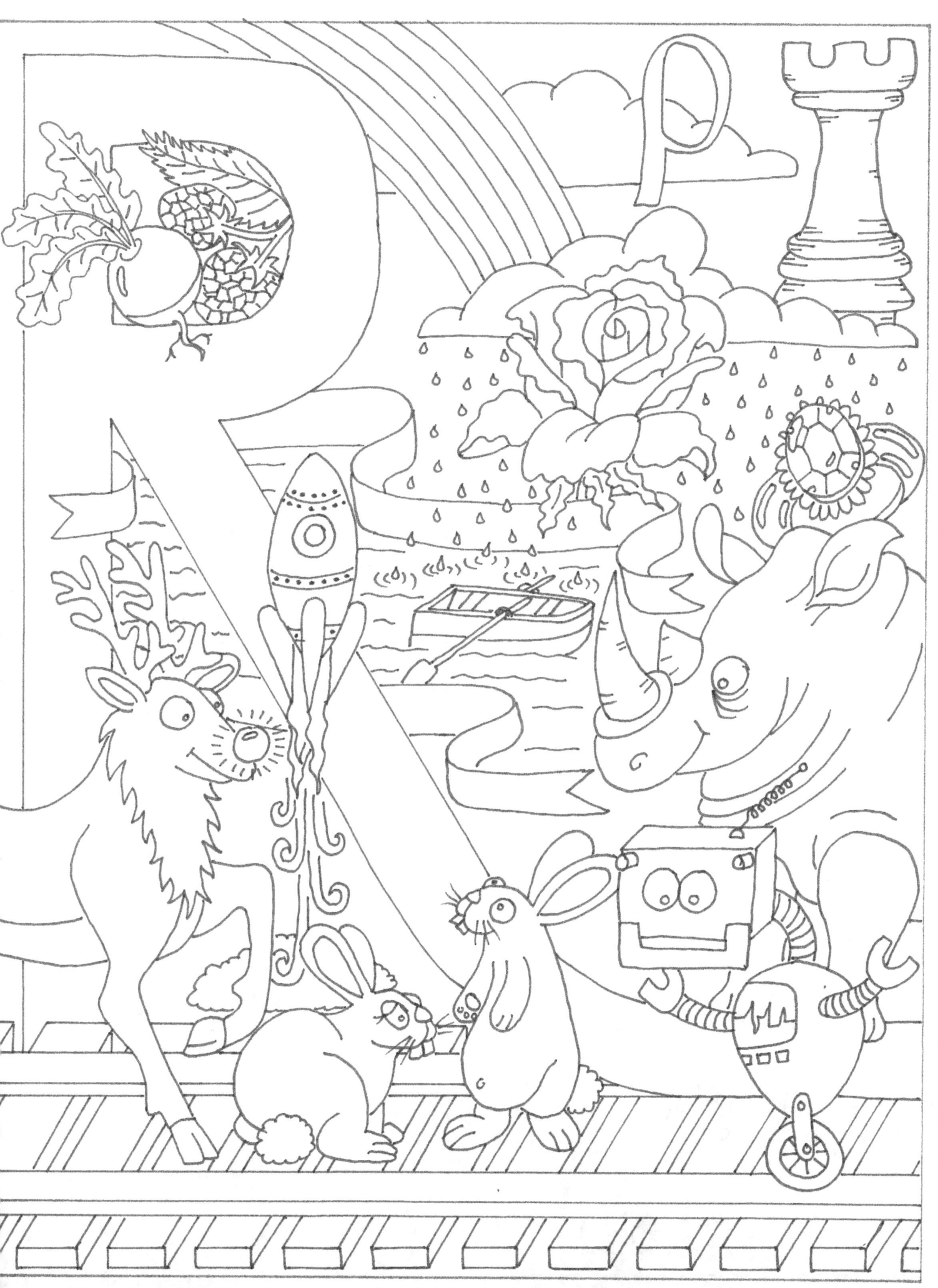

R is for...

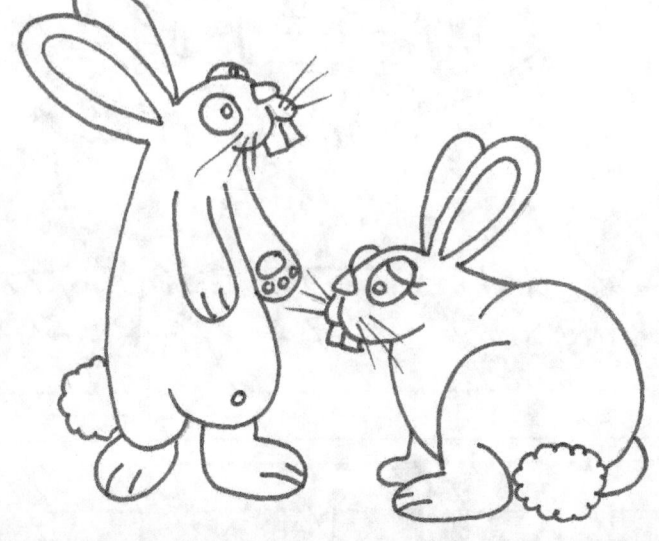

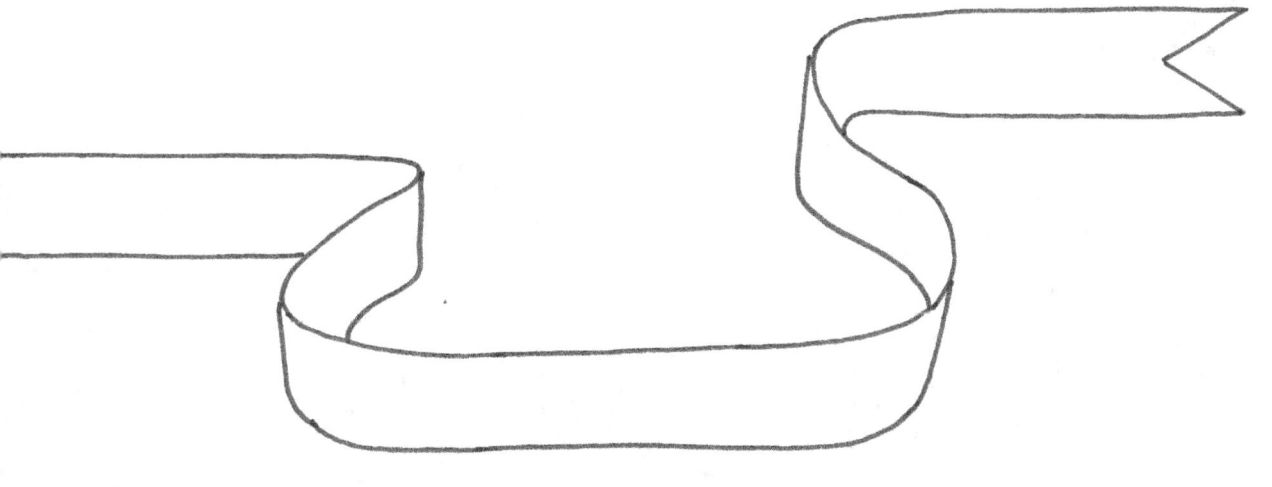

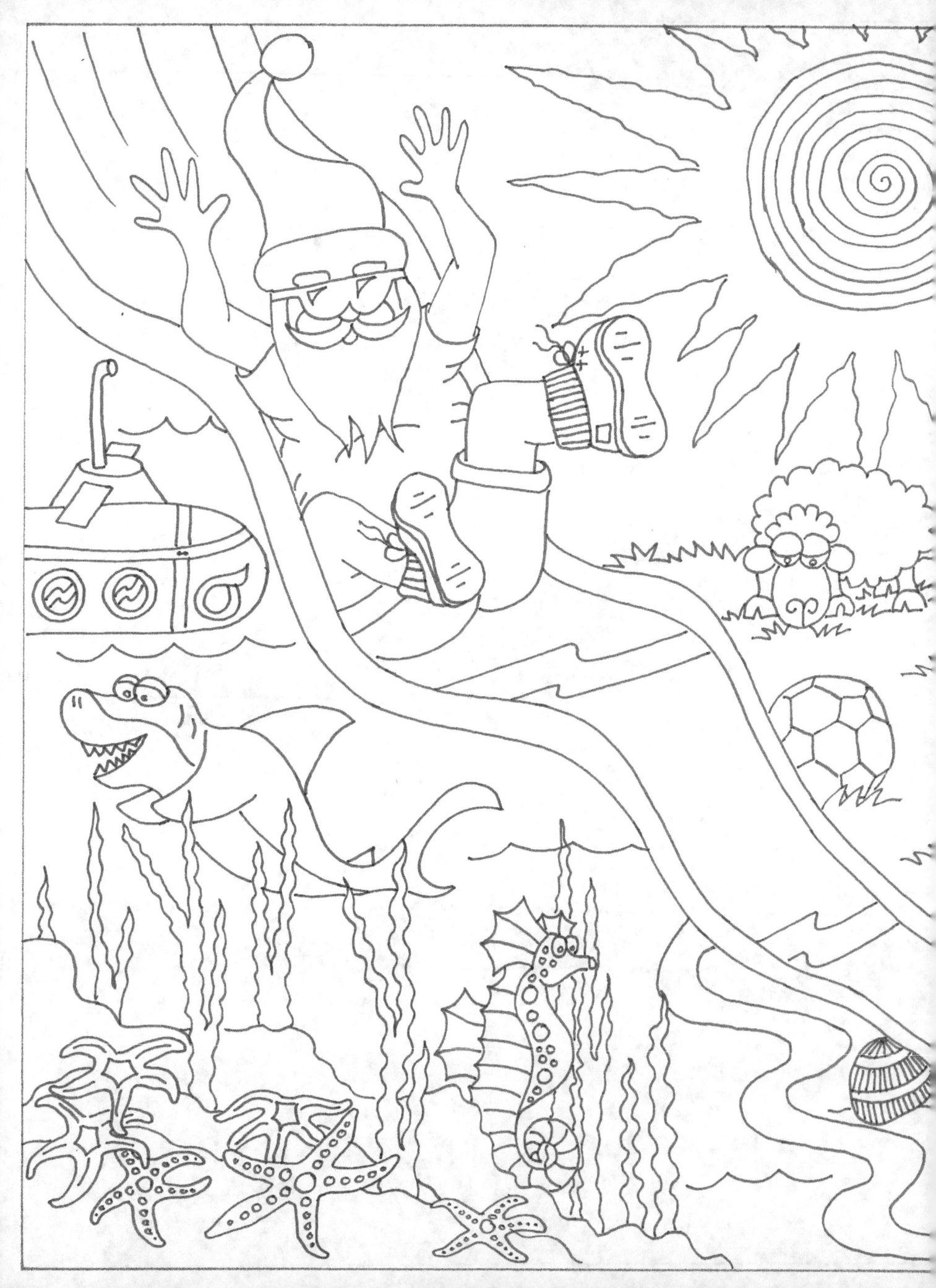

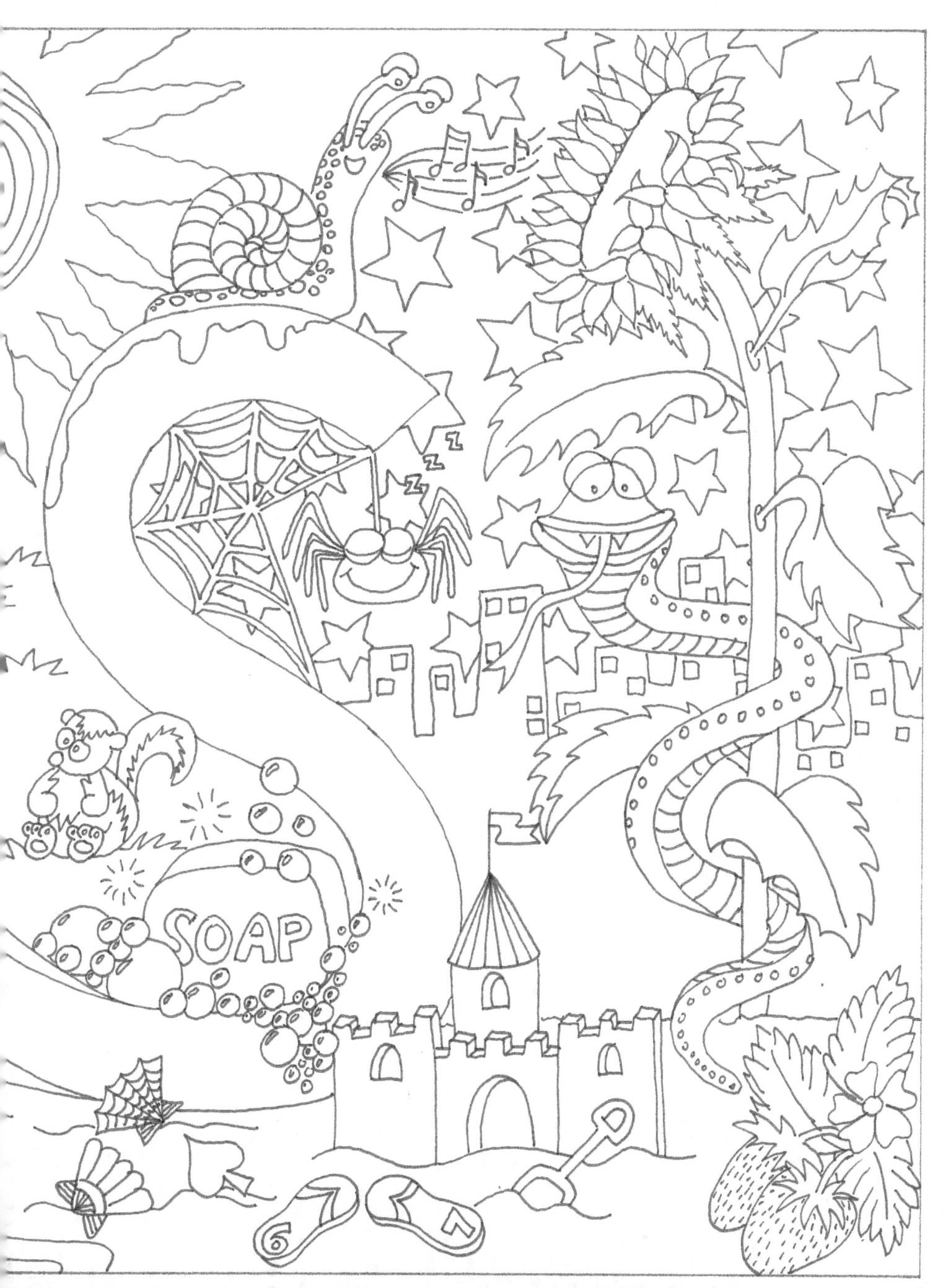

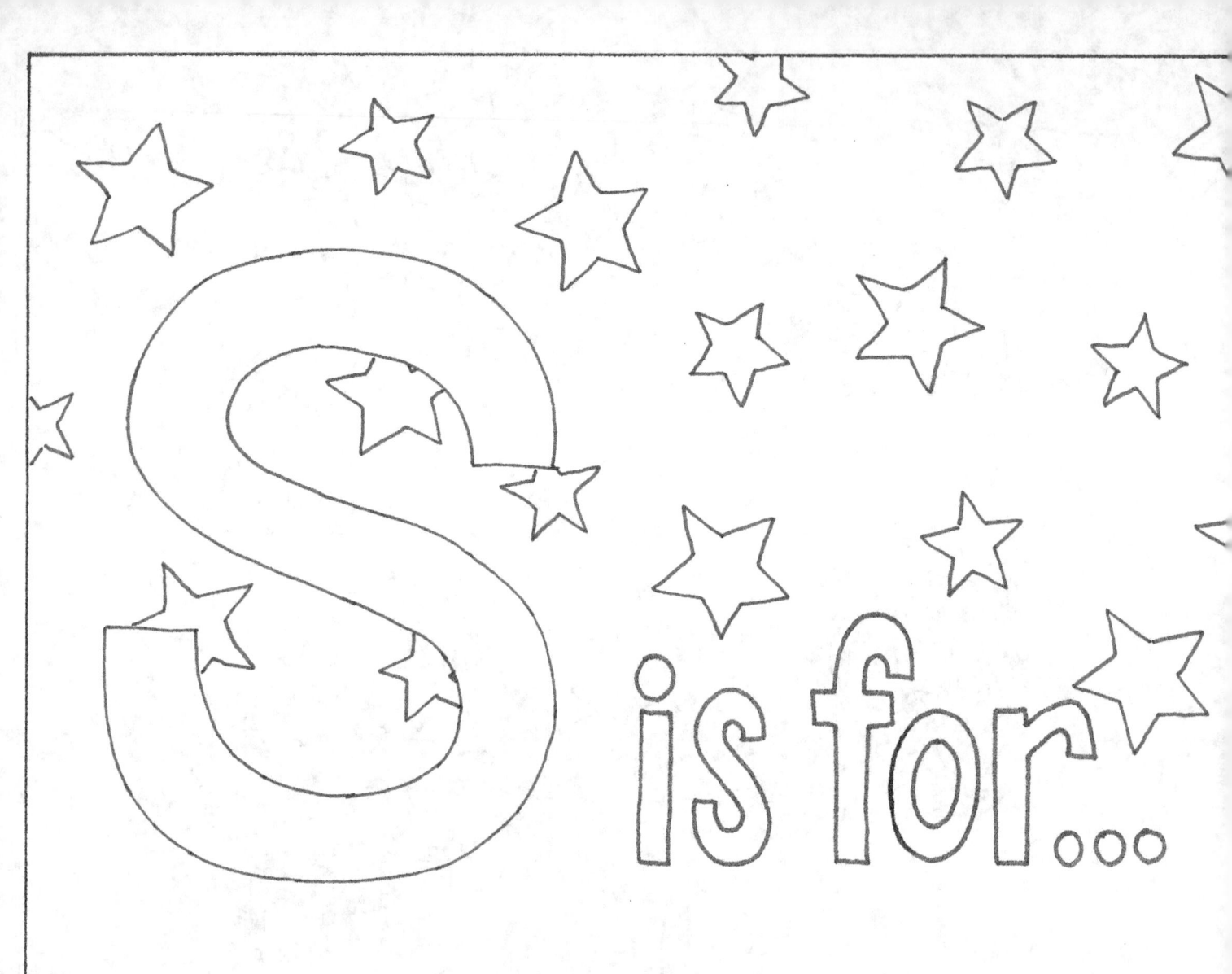

S is for...

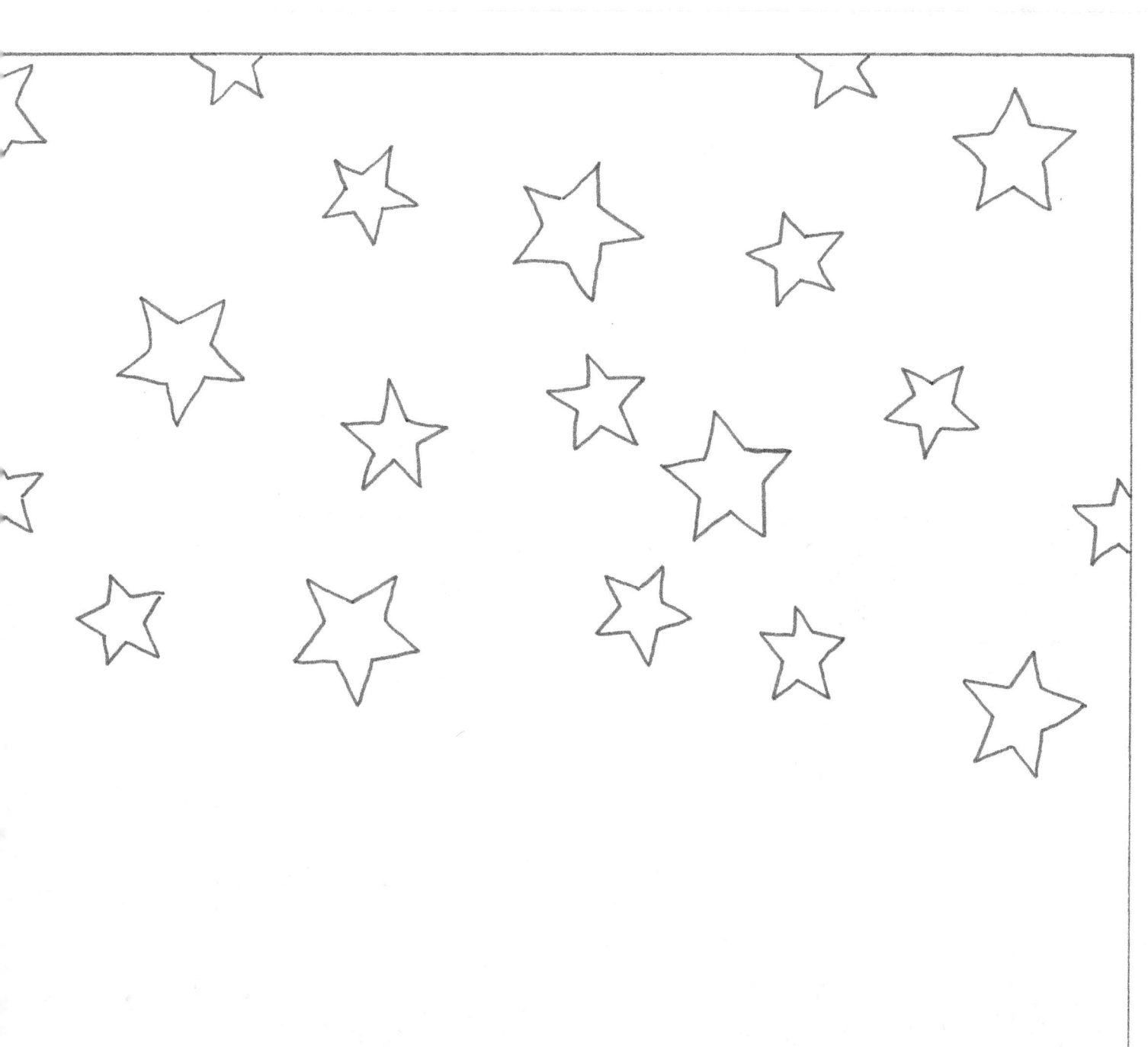

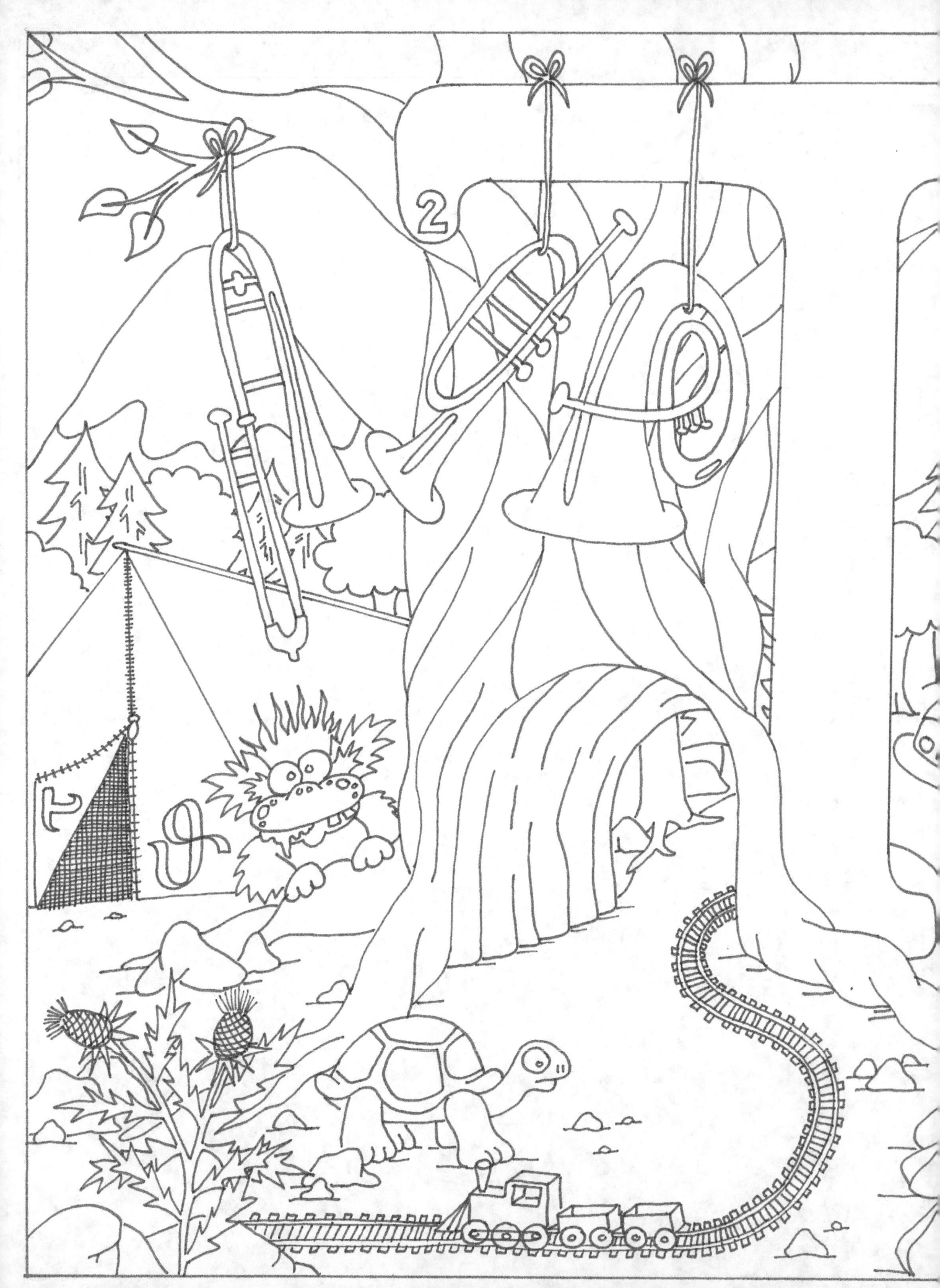

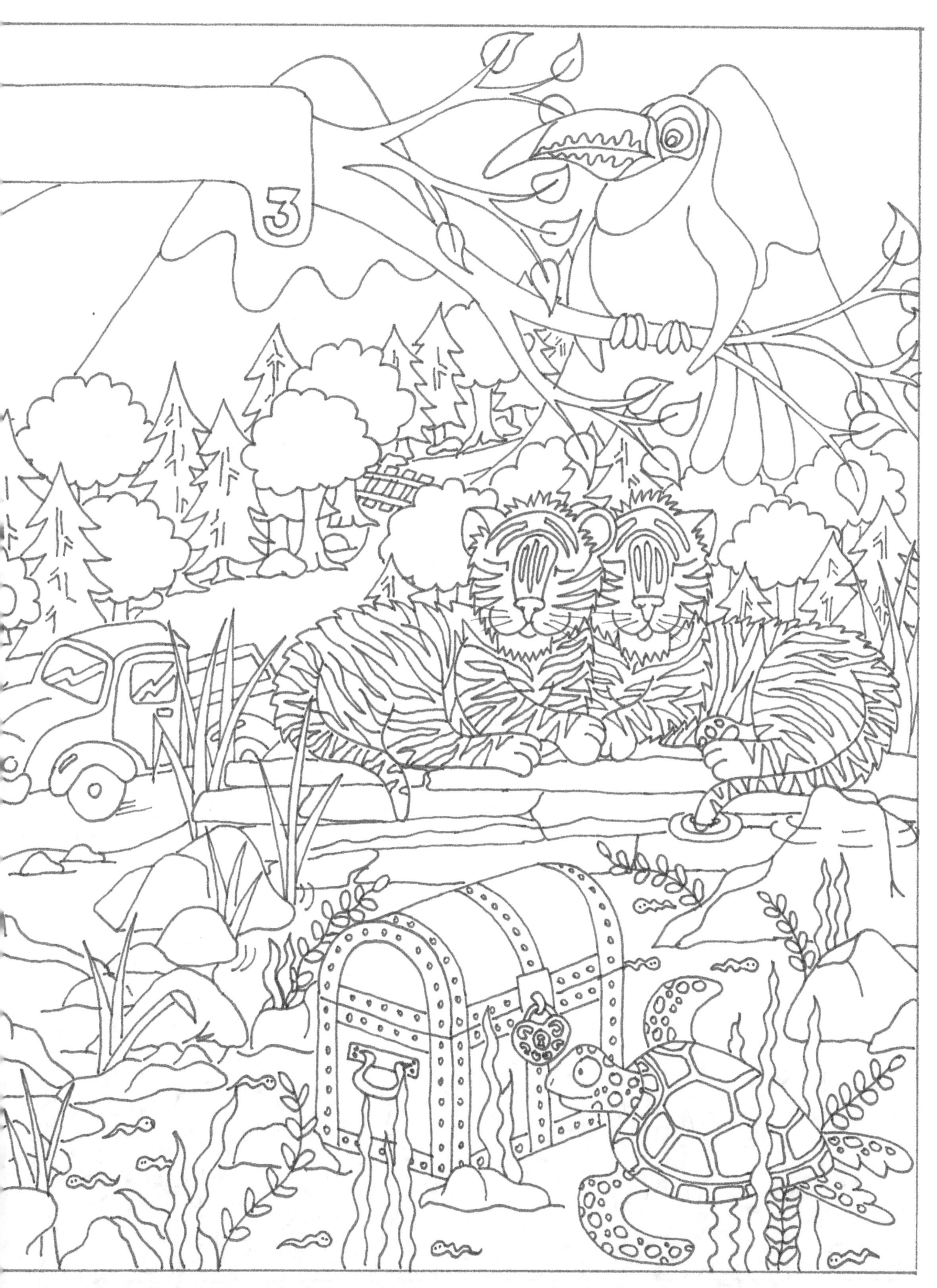

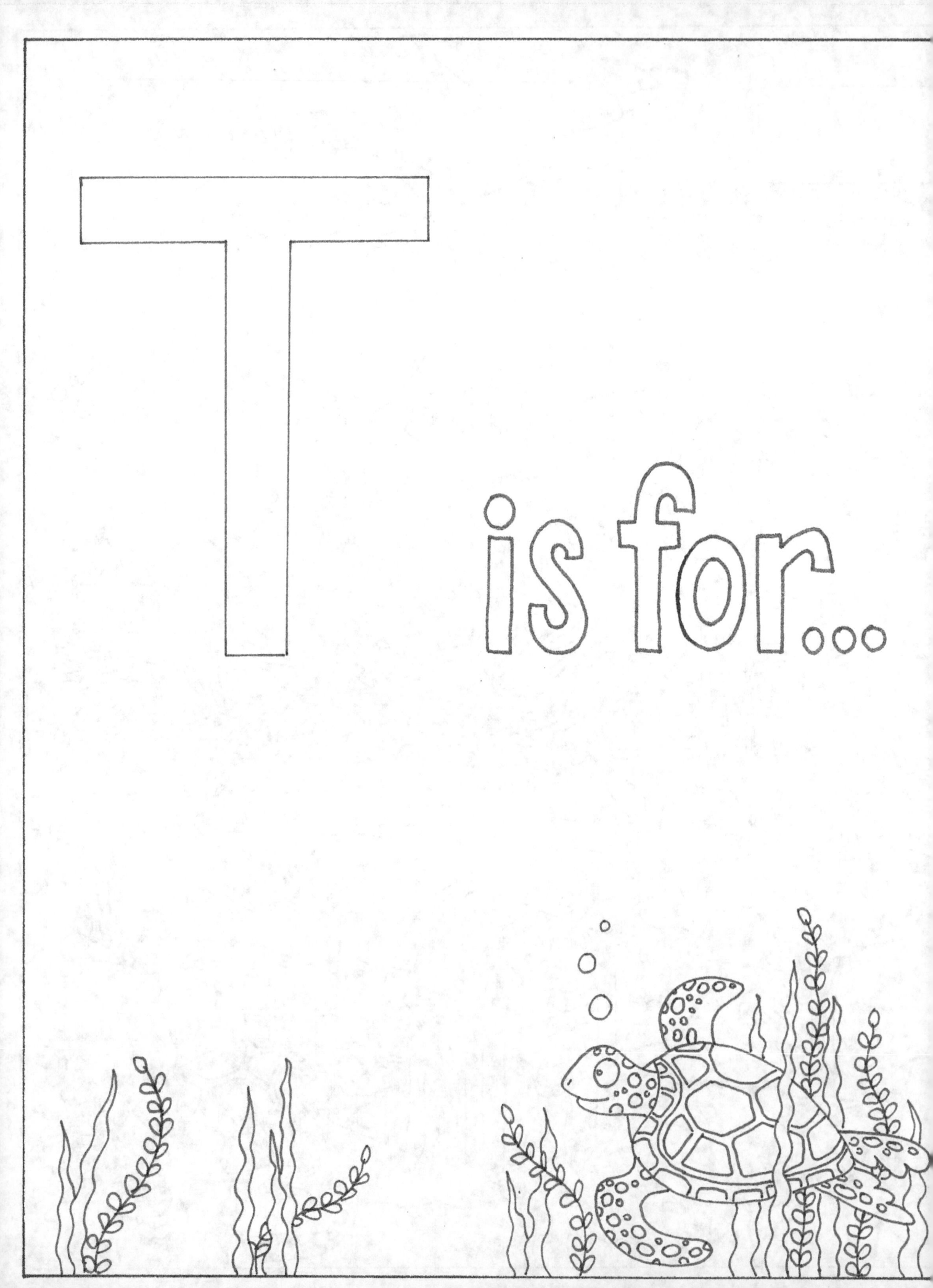

T is for...

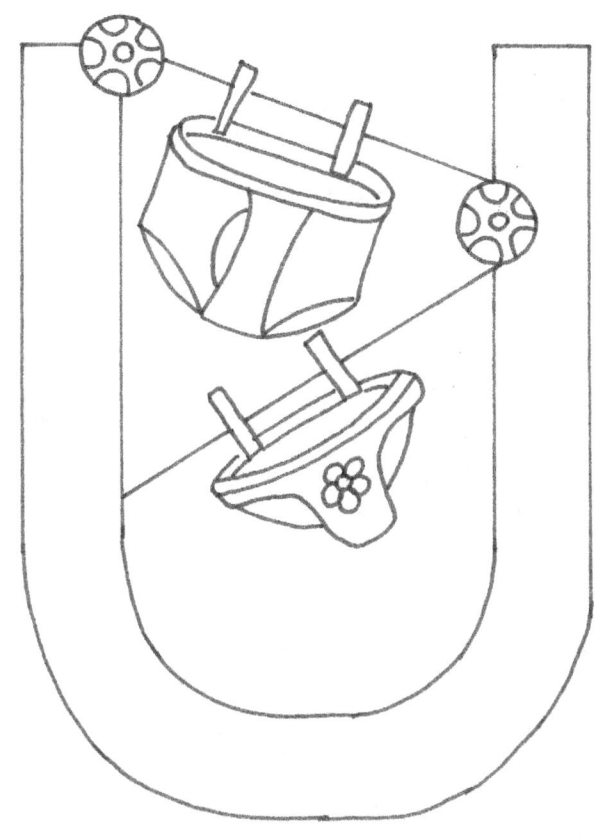

is for...

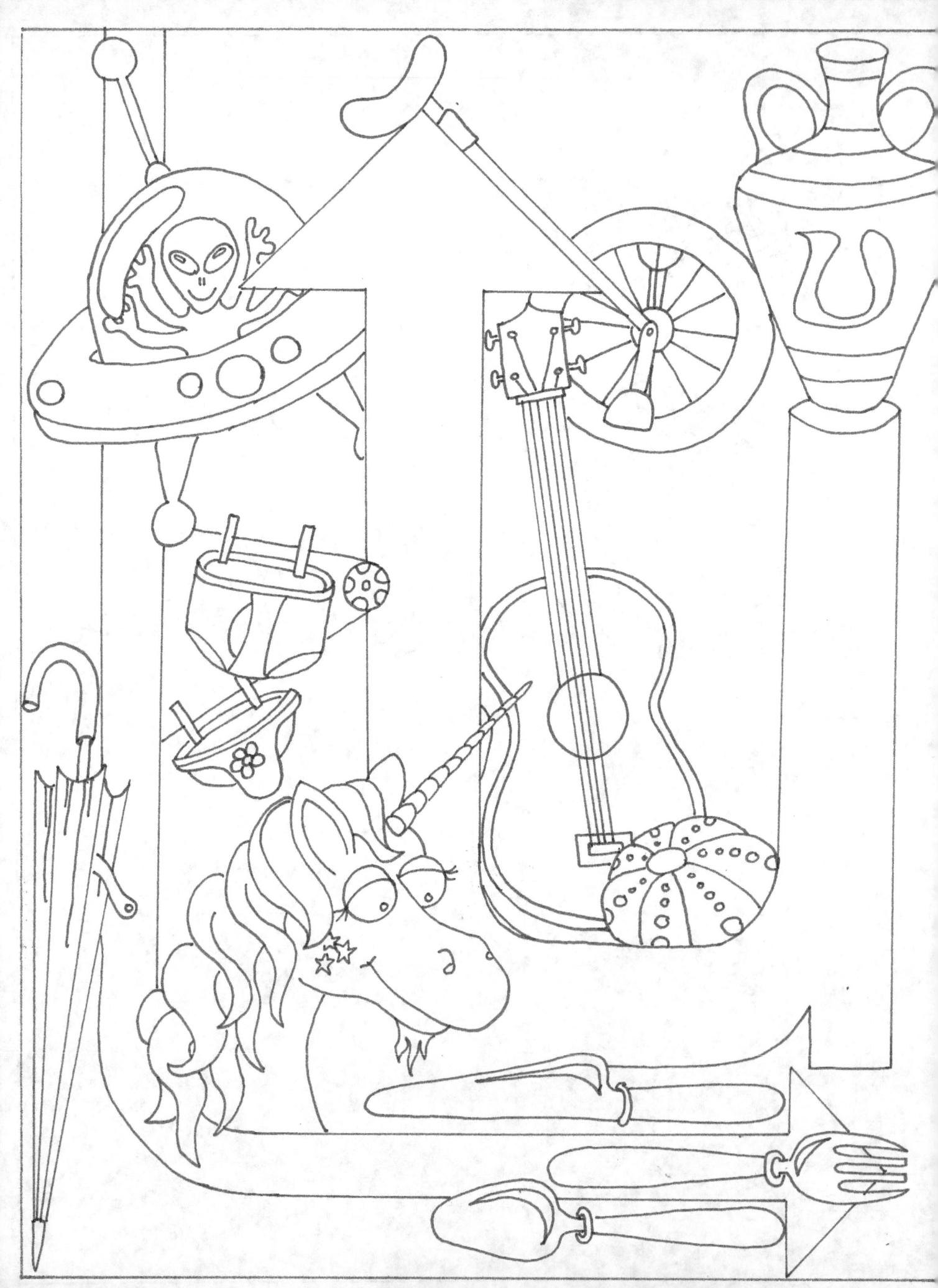

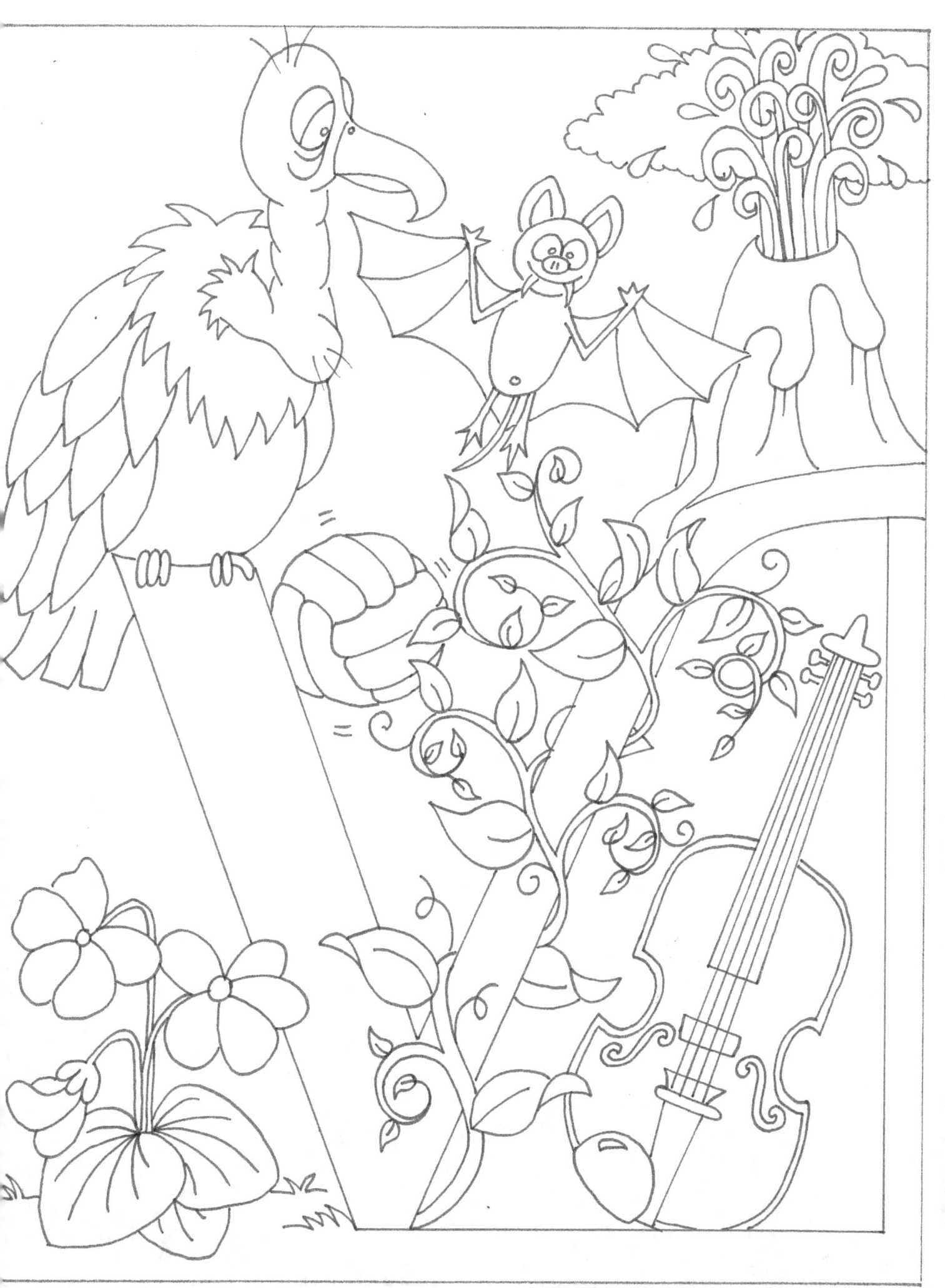

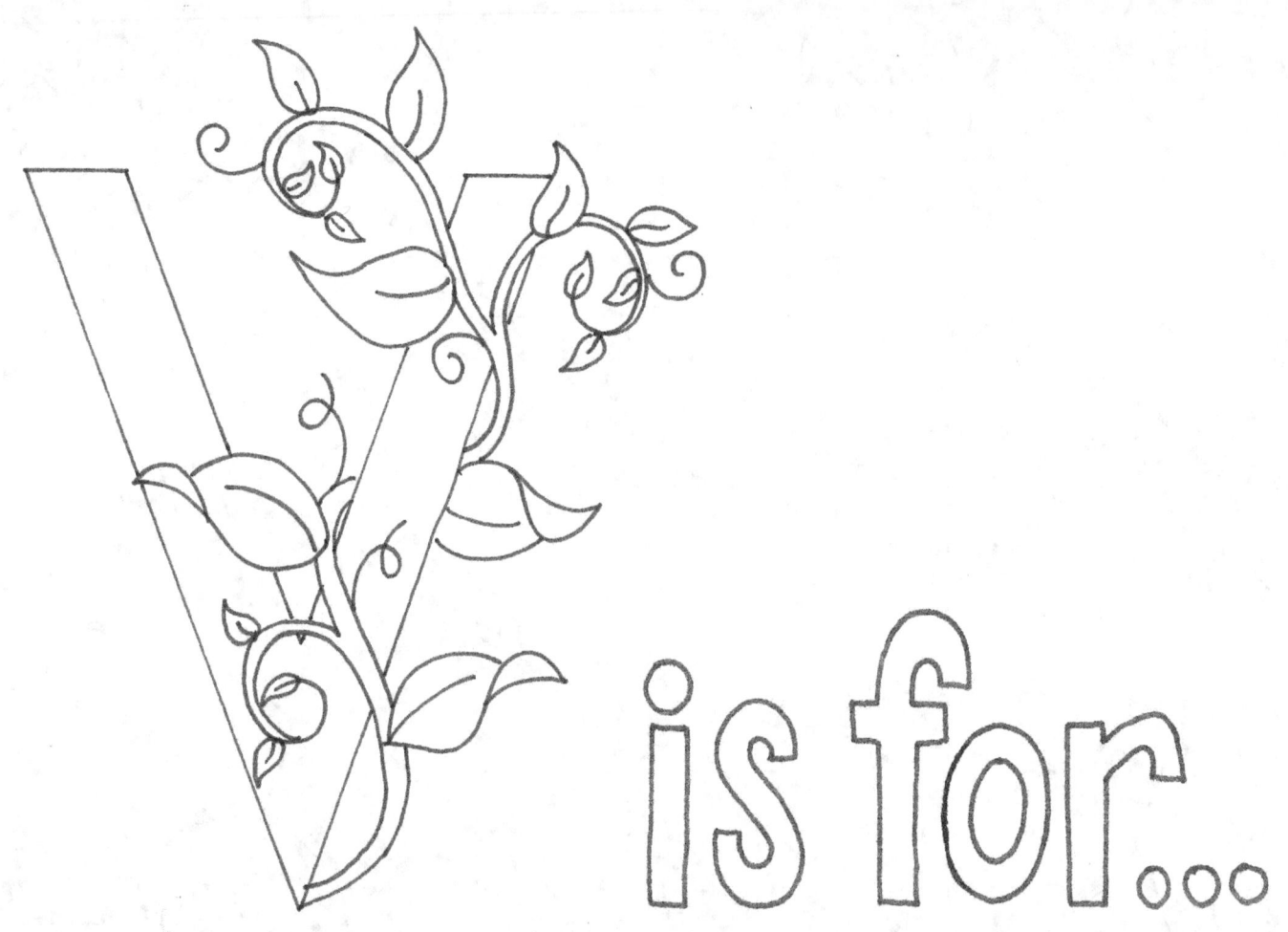

is for...

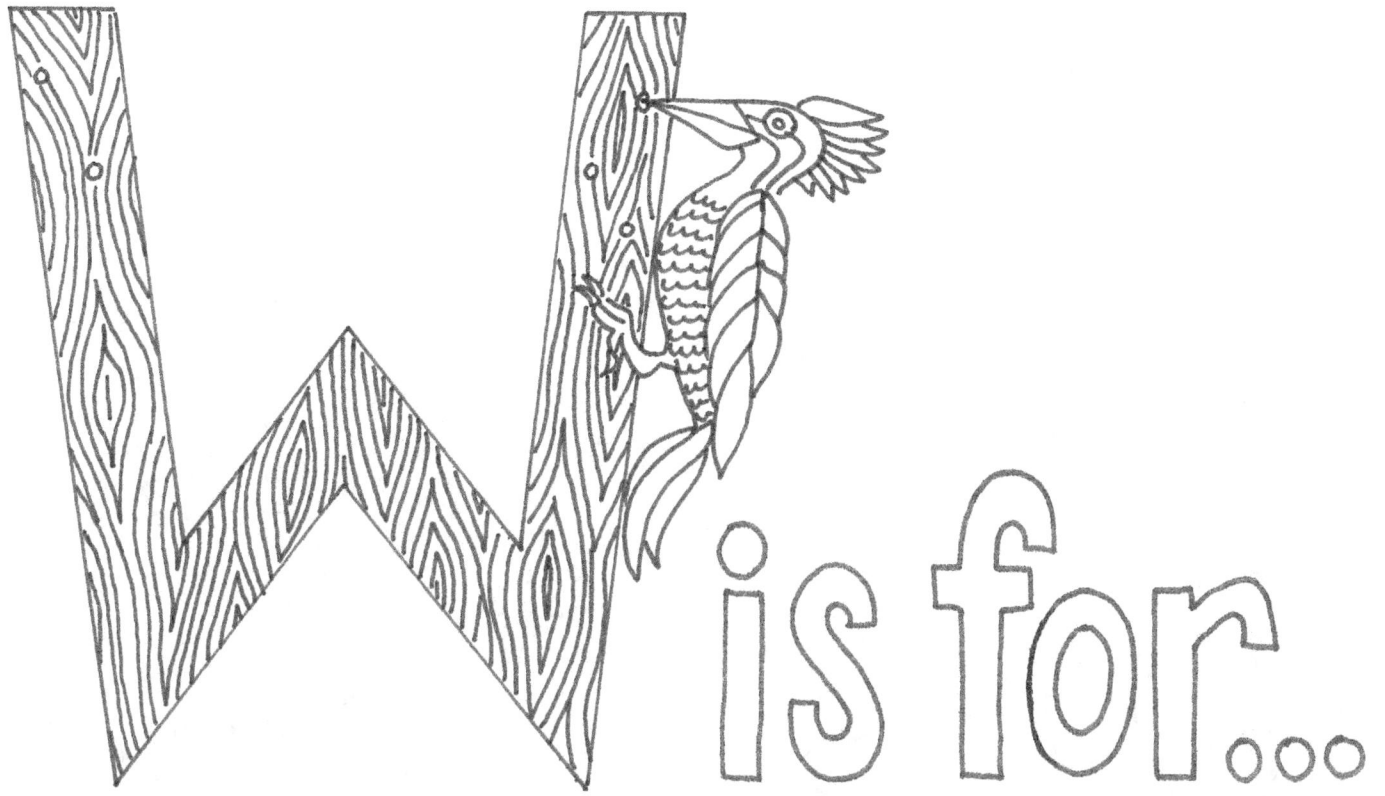

W is for...

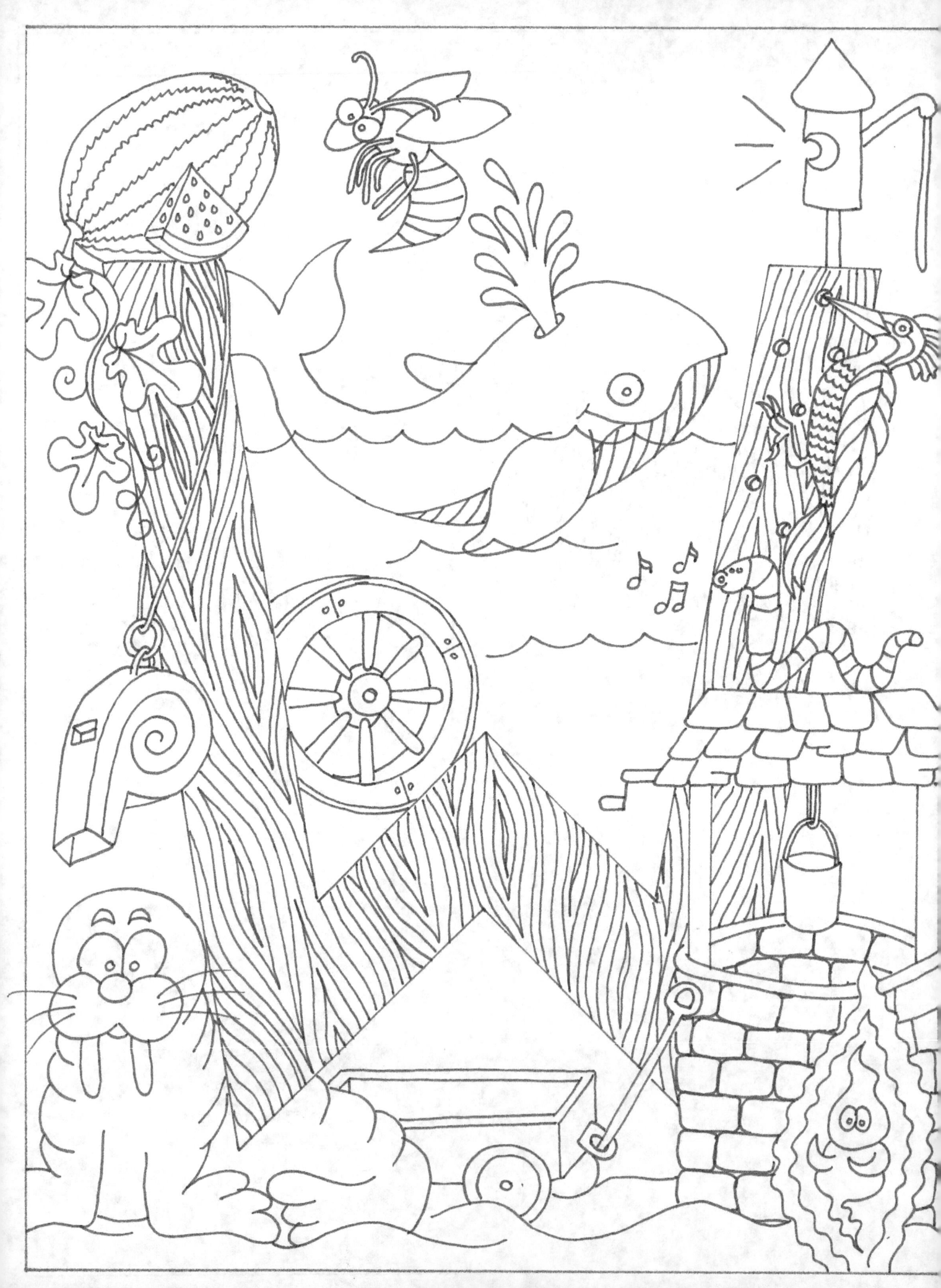

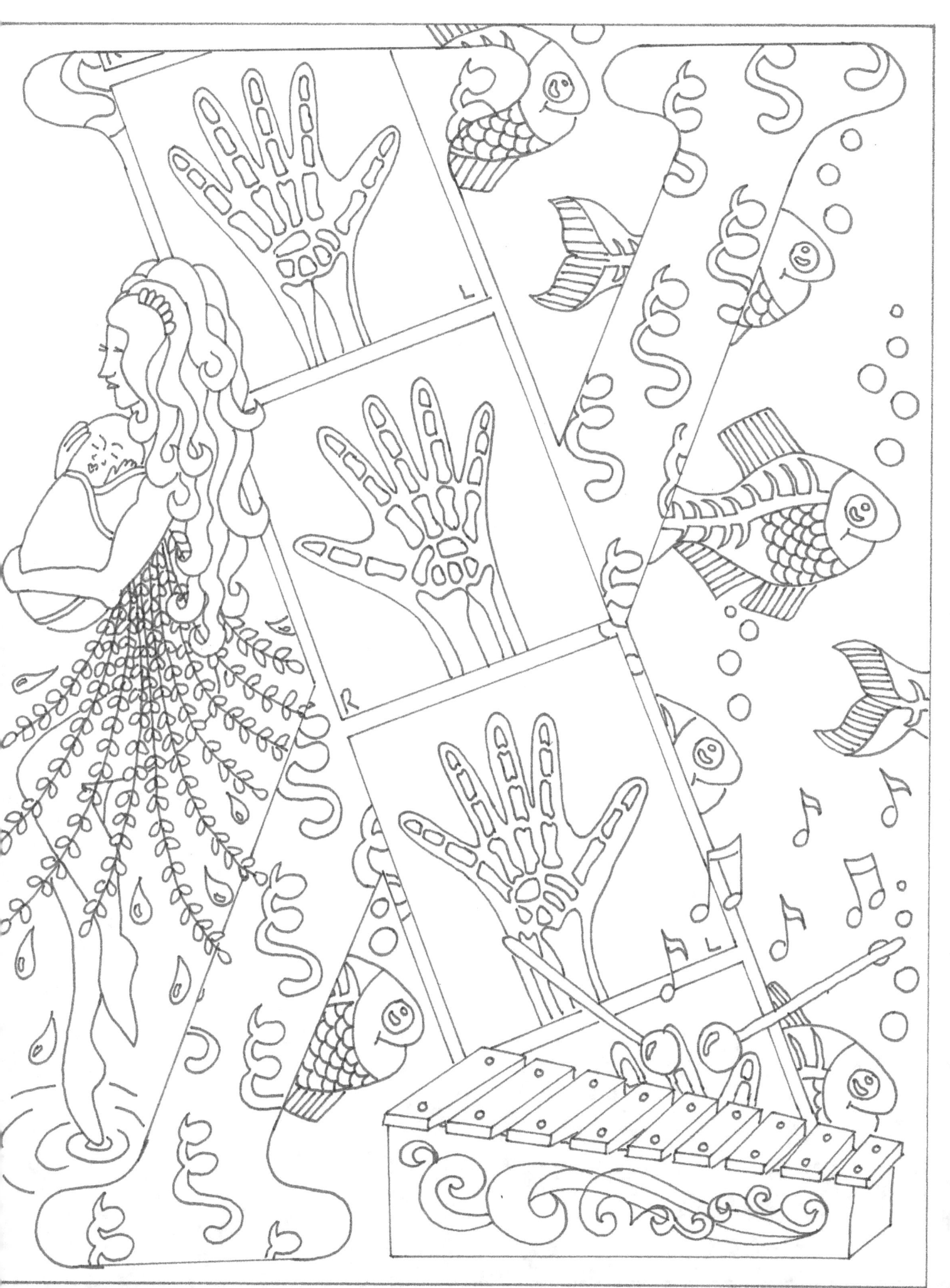

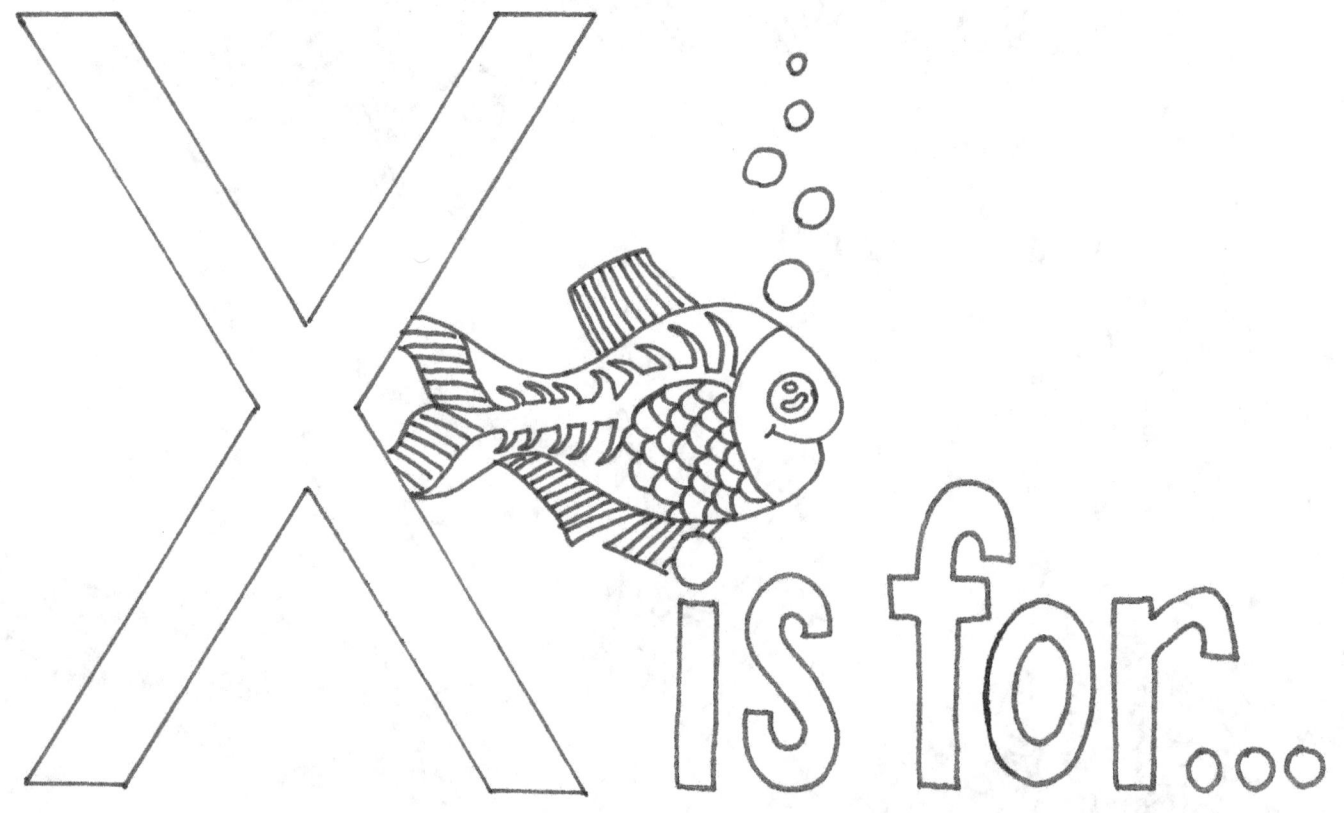

X is for...

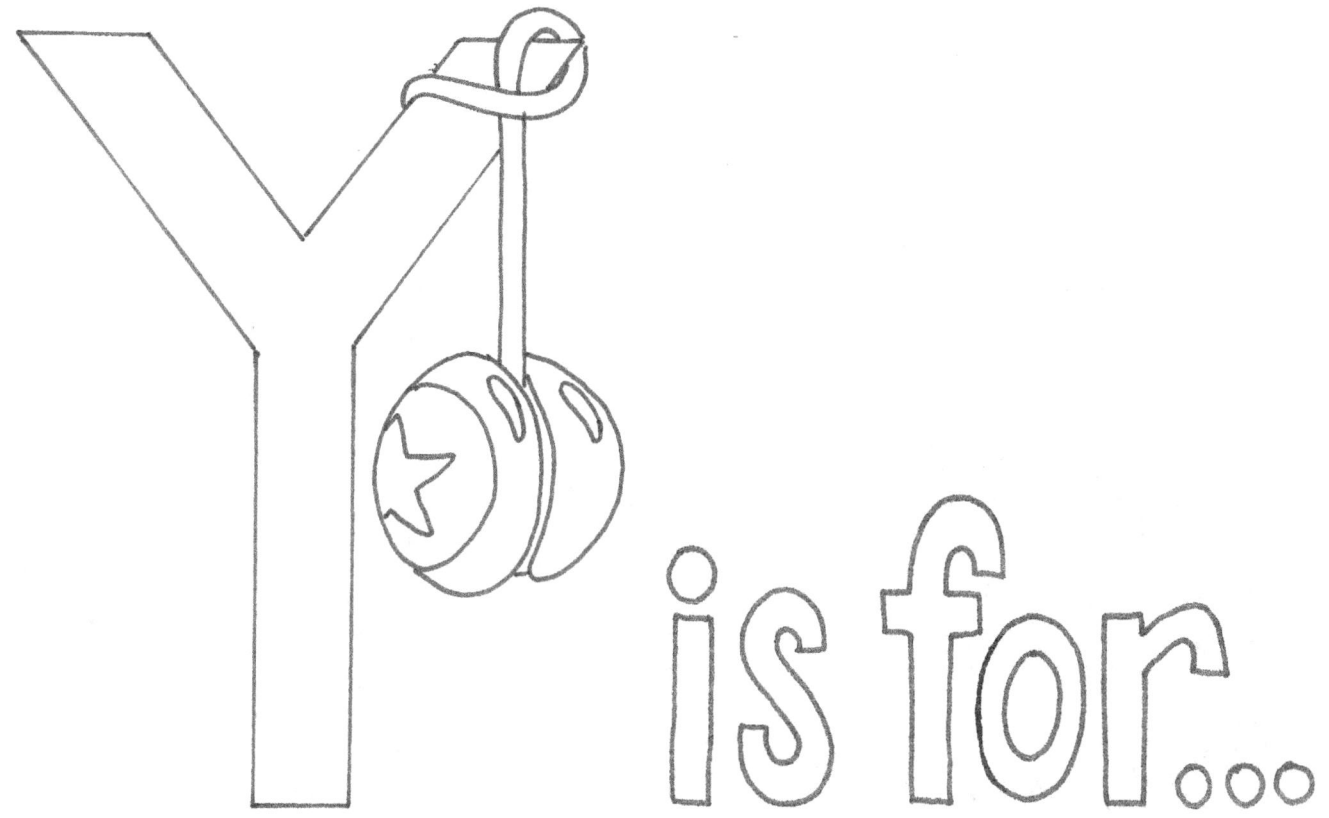

is for...

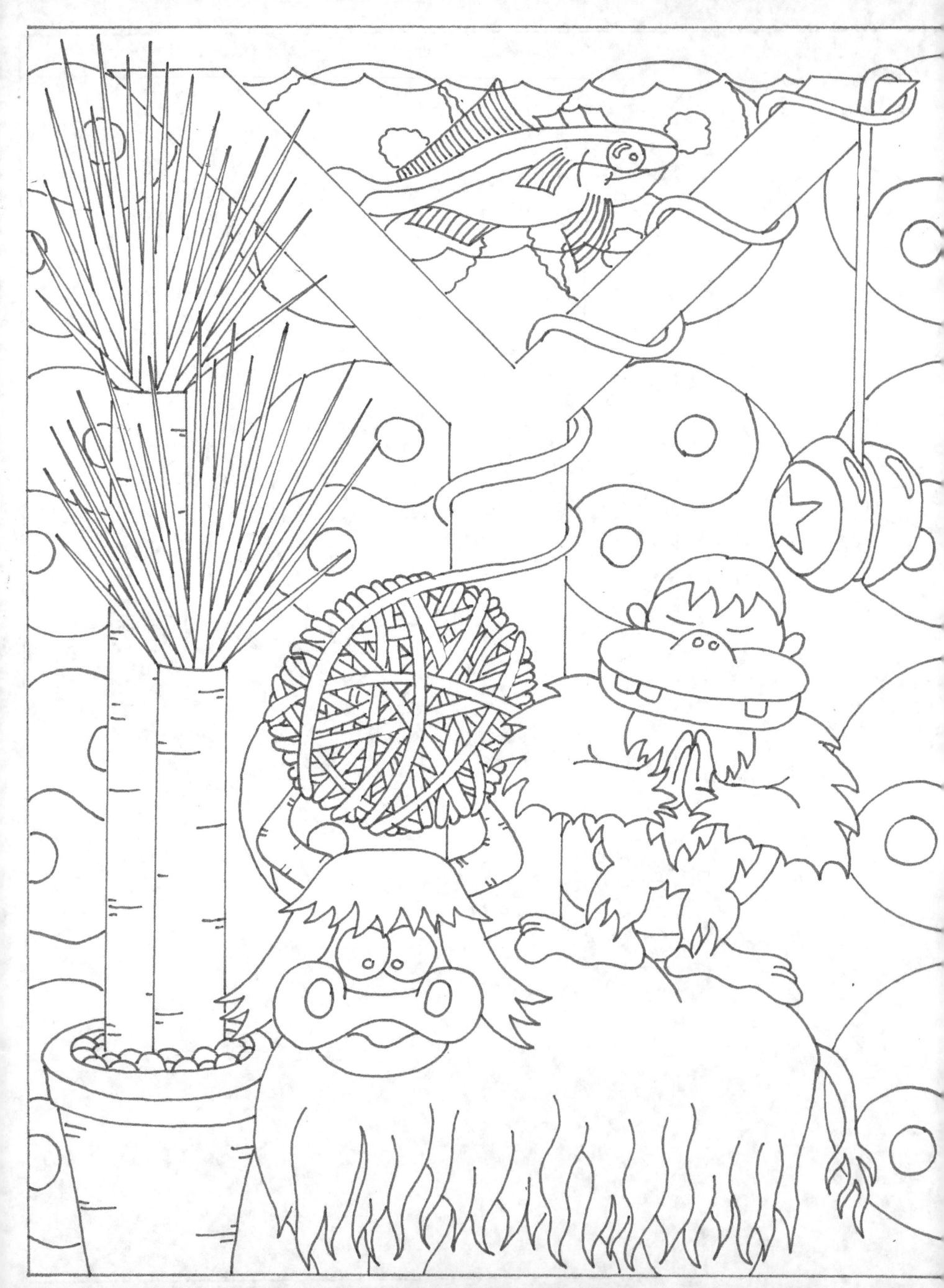

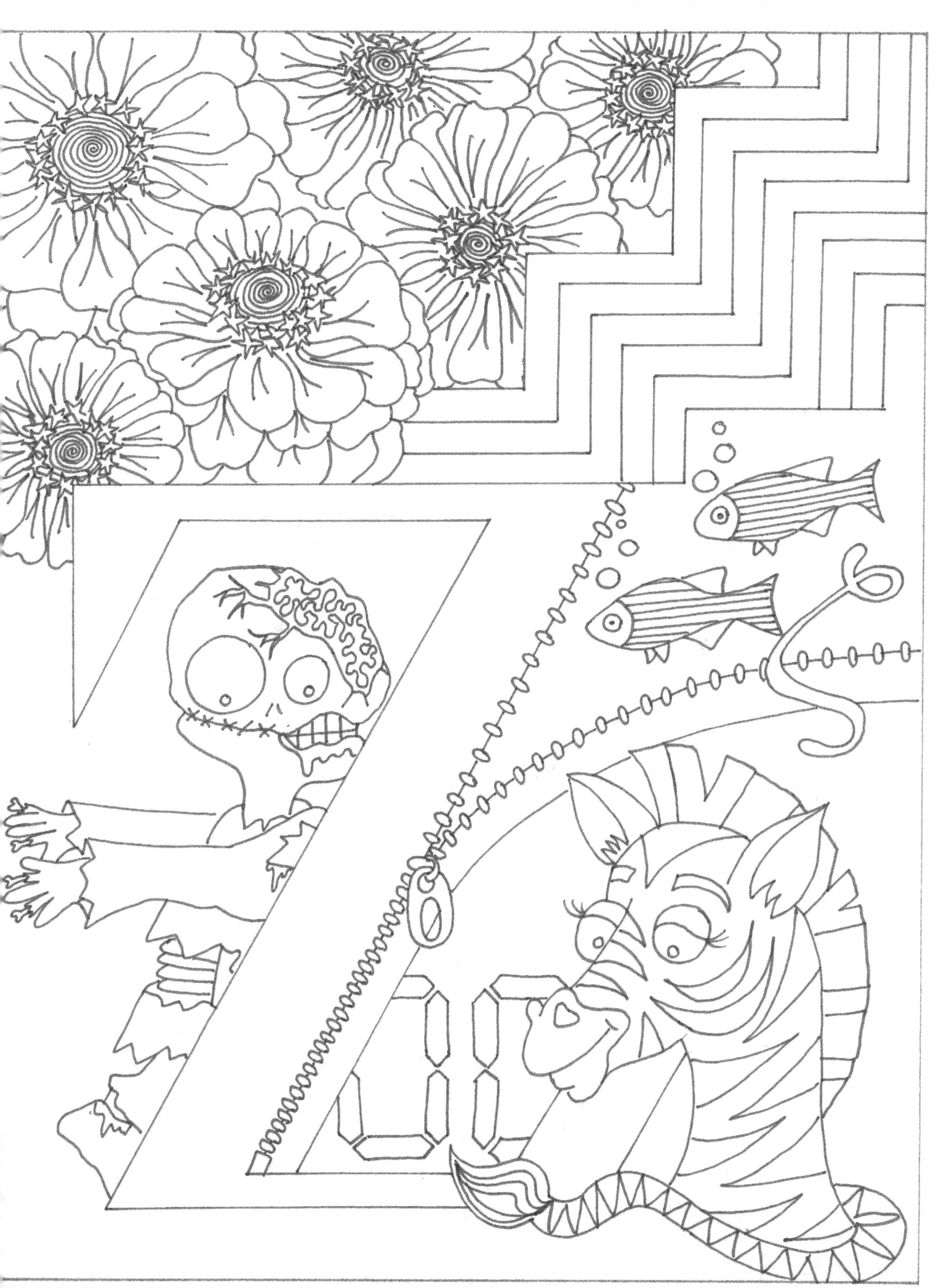

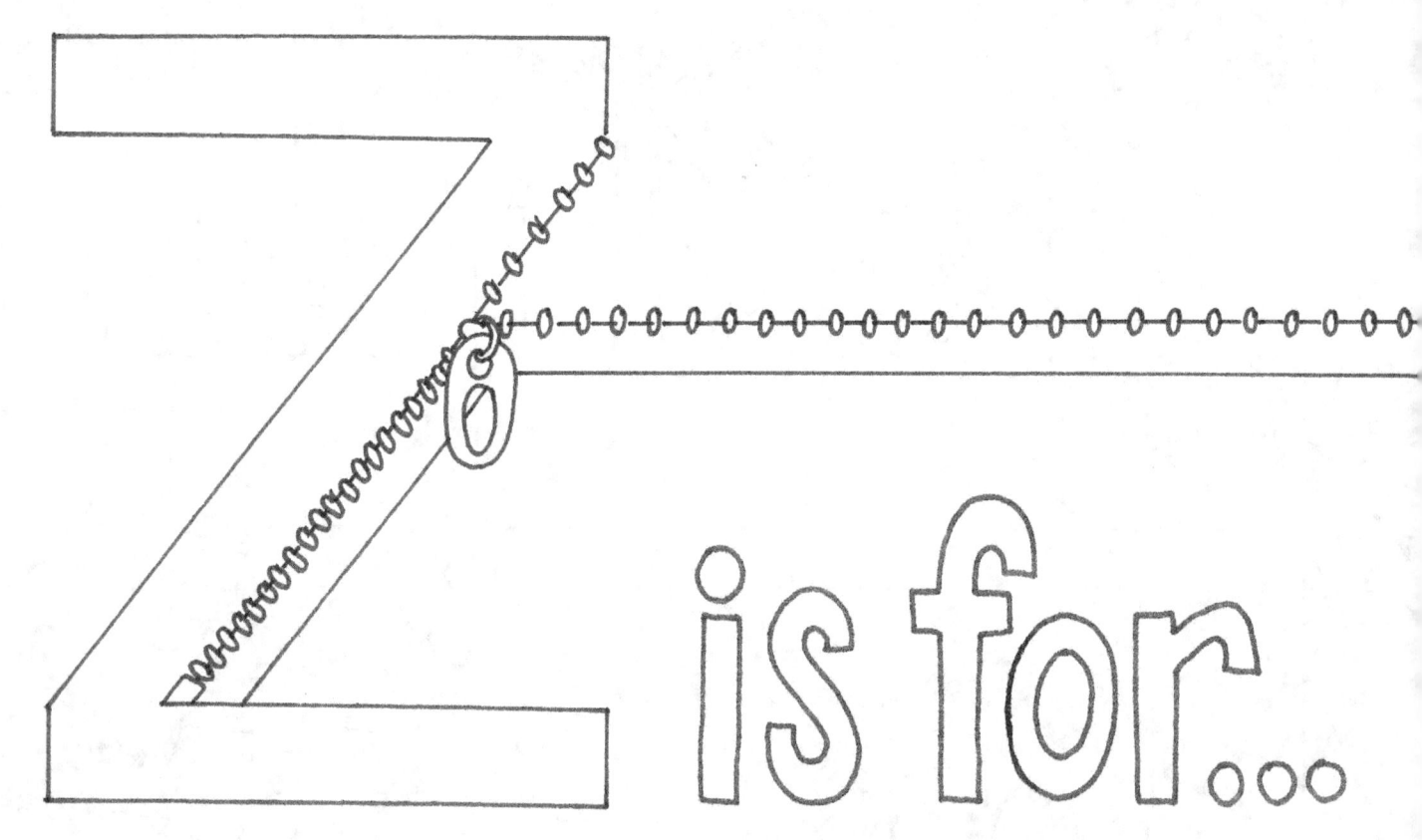

A is for....the legend!

A is for...

Anteater, ants, arrow, ace, aquarium, angel fish, anenome, anchor, accorn, angel, alpha, avacado, alien, arms, axe, airplane, apple, ampersand

B is for...

Book, barn, broom, bale, basket, buoy, birds, bat, branch, bells, bus, butterflies, bees, beaver, banana boat, basketball, beachball, baseball, baseball bat, box, baby blocks, brownie blowing bubbles wearing boots and a button, basking bear on a boulder with balloons, bricks, bishop chess piece, bread, butter, bottles, bridge

C is for...

Castle on a cloud, car, clock, crooked cactus, camel, calico cat curled up on a cozy chair, crochet, curtain, cave, club cards, Chi, carrots, chicken, corn, cow chewing clover, crab, clownfish, catterpiller, coffee cup, cake with cherries and a candle, cobblestone, chimes with coins on chains

D is for...

Daffodil, dragonfly, diamonds, diving dolphin, drum, dutch doll, delta, disco ball, dancing dragon in a dress with a diamond, dapper dinosaur on daisys, dozing dog, drifting dandelion, ducks

E is for...

Electric eel, eagle, ear, earring, eight, earth, eye, elf, elephant, easter eggs, eggplant, envelopes, eta, epsilon,

F is for...

Fennic Fox, fire, fireflys, faint fairy with a fan, flamingo, four, five, ferns, flowers, fence, flies, frog, frogbit, fishes, flute

G is for...

Grapes, gorilla, grass, goldfish, gingerbread, glad gnome playing guitar, gigantic grasshopper, ginko, gladiola, garden, garden gate, giraffes, goose, gamma

H is for...

Hollyhocks, hobbit house in a hill, hoe, hummingbird, hedgehog, haystacks, hind end of a horse holding hemp rope with a heart and horseshoes helping a hippo in a hole, hobo hobbit with a hat, hiding one hand and a hammer in the other, hot air balloons with hearts and herringbone patterns, helicopter, holly, handheld harp, Hawser hitch knot, heron with herring (or halibut!), honey bees, honey, hive and honeycomb

I is for...

Ivy, ink, icicles, iceburg, igloo, iris, iota, iguana, imp with an idea eating icecream

J is for...

Jaguar, jar of jellybeans, jacks, joker, jack, jolly jester juggling jewels on a jug, jam, jellyfish and jelly "J"

K is for...

Kite, koala, kappa, knife, karate kangaroo, knight chess piece, king chess piece, kiss, kneeling king with four king cards, knitting needles, knot, kelpie, kelp, key

L is for...

Ladybug, lock, lance, lady leprechan with laces with luscious lips blowing a kiss for luck holding a lager, ladder on a lighthouse, lightning, laughing lizard, lounging lion, lamda, lotus, lilypad, lily flower, lobster

M is for...

Moose, monicle, monkey, mittens, marrying mice with a mustache under a magnifying glass on a mushroom, moths, moon, mountains, mermaid, mask, mu, map, music – March of the Noble Priests from Magic Flute by Mozart

N is for...

Nightingale, nest, night, naked nymph with a necklace, necktie with notes, net with nails, nu, nautilus, nurse narwal, nine

O is for...

Orange, oak, omega, omicron, ostrich, olive, ogre, octopus, open oven with an owl and onion on it, one

P is for...

Puzzle, police pig, pirate penguin with a parrot, pair of pawns – chess pieces, pumpkin, pineapple, pear, panda, pufferfish in a pond, psi, phi, pi, pie, piano, pencil, pines, prince and princess on a pegasus on a pebble path

Q is for...

Quilt, queen, quail, quahog, quill, question, queen on a quarter, queen of diamonds, queen chess piece

R is for...

Radish, raspberry, rainbow, rain, rho, rook chess piece, rose, ruby ring, rhino, ribbon river, rowboat, rocket, Rudolph the red nosed reindeer, rabbits, robot riding the rails on a railroad

S is for...

Submarine, sigma, smiling shark, seaweed, starfish, seahorse, seashore, shells, spade, sandels, six, seven, sandcastle, shovel, strawberry, snake slithering up the sunflower stalk, stars over a skyline, sleeping spider, singing snail leaving slime, sun, sheep, skunk, soccer ball, soap, sliding Santa in shorts, shirt, shoes, socks and sunglasses

T is for...

Tired twin tigers, treasure chest, turtle, ten tadpoles, troll, tent, tao, theda, tunnel in a tall tree, thistle, tortoise, tuba, trombone, trumpet tied to a tree or a "t", toucan, toy train, truck with tires, tons of trees, two, three, train tracks

U is for...

UFO, underwear, umbrella, unicorn, ukelele, urchin, unicycle, urn, upsilon, utencils, up and under

V is for...

Vulture, vampire bat, volcano, vine, violin (or viola), violet, volleyball

W is for...

Watermelon, wasp, whale, whistle, water, wheel, steam whistle, walrus, wagon, wishing well, will'o'the'wisp, whistling worm, woodpecker, woodgrain

X is for...

X-ray, x-ray fish, xylaphone, xu, Xana

Y is for...

YingYang, yoyo, yellowfin, yarn, yoga Yeti, yak, yucca

Z is for...

Zombie, zipper, zebra, zebrafish, zero's , word "Zoo", zeta, zinnia

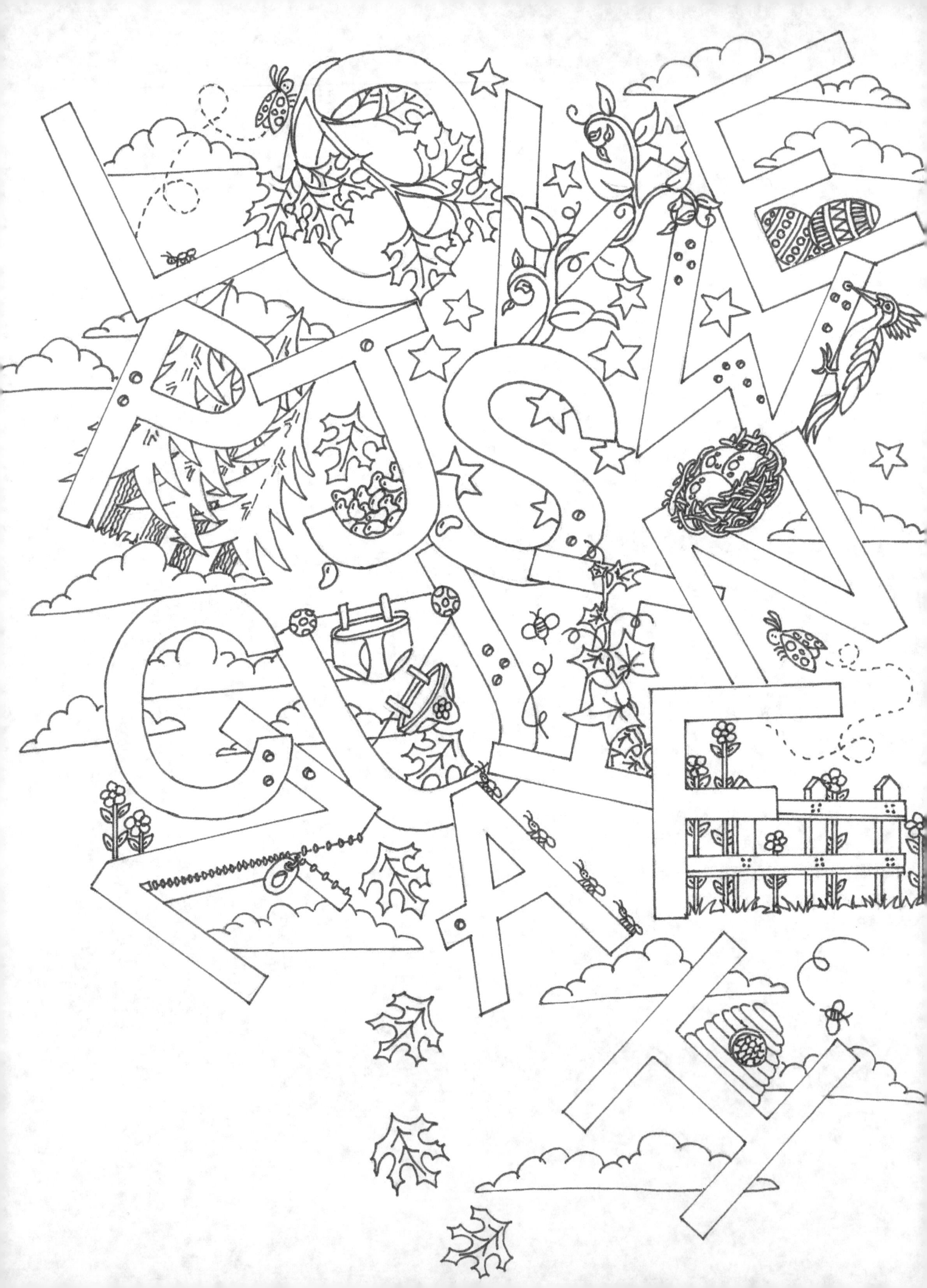